The
English Ritual

THE

ENGLISH RITUAL

THE BOOK OF ADMINISTRATION OF

THE SACRAMENTS

AND OTHER

RITES AND CEREMONIES OF THE CHURCH

WITH AN INTRODUCTION BY

JULIEN CHILCOTT-MONK

CANTERBURY
PRESS
Norwich

Qui enim bene ministraverint, gradum bonum sibi acquirent.

1 TIM. iii. 13.

Text © Tufton Books 2002
Introduction © Julien Chilcott-Monk 2002

First published by W. Knott and Son Ltd, London
This new edition published in 2002 by the Canterbury Press Norwich
St Mary's Works, St Mary's Plain
Norwich, Norfolk, NR3 3BH
by permission of the copyright holders,
Tufton Books (a Church Union imprint), Tufton Street, London

British Library Cataloguing in Publication data

A catalogue record for this book is available
from the British Library

ISBN 1-85311-457-X

Printed in Great Britain by
Biddles, Ltd, Guildford and King's Lynn

INTRODUCTION

IT IS MOST APPROPRIATE that this companion to *The English Missal* is now reissued. The *Missal* itself appeared again last year after an absence of forty years or so. *The English Ritual* has been longer in the reprinting.

Part I contains the forms for the 'Occasional' Rites according to (1) the Western Use for England and (2) The Book of Common Prayer. Very helpfully, the Western Rites are printed in dark type and those of The Book of Common Prayer in lighter type, so that either form may easily be distinguished. It is most useful to have these Rites side-by-side.

Part II is replete with Blessings. And here we come across the Blessing of a Domestic Oratory and it reminds us immediately of how much we have lost in recent decades. Even though icons, crucifixes and statues are readily available, the altarless oratory or holy place – beloved of the Orthodox Christian – is not likely to be encouraged in the Church of England these days. Doubtless, such a place would be regarded as 'dangerous' – a word, incidentally, employed recently by an archdeacon in refusing a request for the installation of an additional side-altar in a parish church!

Simply, the holy place can take the form of a statue or icon here, a crucifix there. It can be something more elaborate, set up, say, in an attic – a gradine with frontal, adorned with candles and crucifix before which a daily office or the rosary can be recited. Of course, these aids are not essential; they are simply aids. Prayer can be made concurrently with any domestic task and, indeed, the task itself can be made into prayer without such aids. However, there is undoubtedly a place for the holy place. Recently, a priest friend of mine advocated the placing of a statue of the Sacred Heart upon the television, facing the viewer. Unsuitable viewing would soon be turned into a holy place!

This digression is a consequence of reading that one short blessing. What other possibilities for contemplation lie in wait for the reader and worshipper?

In the Appendix are contained more prayers, litanies and a miscellany of devotions. Most will insert 'Blessed be her Glorious Assumption' in The Divine Praises (page 223), and that is easily done, and most will be unable to resist the wonderful prayer which begs the prayers of the Saints: 'O Merciful God, let the glorious intercession of thy Saints assist us ... Be mindful of our fathers, Eleutherius, Celestine and Gregory ... Remember our holy martyrs ... especially our first martyr, Saint Alban, and thy most glorious bishop, Saint Thomas of Canterbury. Remember all those holy confessors ... holy monks ... holy virgins and widows, who made this once an island of Saints, illustrious by their glorious merits and virtues ...' Ah, what a source of supply for hours of meditation. A cry from the heart, indeed.

Julien Chilcott-Monk
St Michael the Archangel 2001

THE

CONTENTS OF THIS BOOK.

PART I.

PART II.

APPENDIX.

THE ENGLISH RITUAL
PART I.

ORDER OF BAPTISM OF CHILDREN
According to the Western Rite.

When the Sacrament of Baptism is to be admin-istered, the following things must be made ready :—

1. *Vessels of the sacred Oil of Catechumens, and Chrism.*

2. *A Vessel with salt, either already blessed or to be blessed.*

3. *A Vessel or shell of silver or other metal, for pouring the water of Baptism on the head of the person to be baptized.*

4. *A bason to receive water which flows from off the head.*

5. *Cotton wool or the like to wipe the places anointed with the sacred Oil.*

6. *Two stoles, one violet and the other white, or at least one.*

7. *Bread crumbs and a vessel with water to wash the Priest's hands.*

8. *A white linen cloth, to be placed on the Child's head.*

9. *A wax candle, to be delivered burning to the baptized.*

10. *The* ENGLISH RITUAL *and the Baptismal Register.*

All things being duly prepared, the Priest, having washed his hands, comes, vested in surplice and violet stole, with one or more Clerks, likewise vested in surplice, and at the threshold of the Church, awaits those who bring the Child to Baptism.

AT THE DOORS OF THE CHURCH.

The Priest, having ascertained the name(s), questions the Child (if several are to be baptized, each separately):

N. **What dost thou ask of the Church of God?**

The Godfather answers : **Faith.**

Priest. **What doth Faith bring thee to?**

℞. **Life everlasting.**

Priest (also separately to each):

2. **If then thou desirest to enter into life, keep the commandments.   Thou shalt love the Lord thy God, with thy whole heart, with thy whole soul, and with thy whole mind ; and thy neighbour as thyself.**

3. *Then he blows three times gently into the face of the Child, and says once (separately to each):*

Go out of . him, thou unclean spirit, and give place unto the Holy Spirit the Paraclete.

4. *Then he makes with his thumb the sign of the Cross on the forehead and on the breast of the Child, saying (separately to each):*

Receive the sign of the Cross both in thy fore ✠ head and in thy he ✠ art, take the faith of heavenly precepts : and be thou such in thy conversation, that thou mayest now be the temple of God.

For one.

Let us pray.   *Collect.*

WE beseech thee, O Lord, graciously hear our prayers : and keep with thy perpetual power this thine Elect *N.,* who hath been signed with the sign of the Cross of the Lord : that *he,* keeping the rudiments of the greatness of thy glory, may by observing of thy commandments be worthy to attain unto the glory of regeneration. Through Christ, our Lord.

℞. Amen.

For several.

Let us pray.   *Collect.*

WE beseech thee, O Lord, graciously hear our prayers : and keep with thy perpetual power these thine Elect *N.* and *N.,* who have been signed with the sign of the Cross of the Lord : that they, keeping the rudiments of the greatness of thy glory, may by observing of thy commandments be worthy to attain unto the glory of regeneration.   Through Christ, our Lord.

℞. Amen.

5. *Then he places his hand upon the head of the Child, and afterwards holding his hand extended, he says :*

5. *Then he places his hand upon the heads of the Children, and afterwards holding his hand extended, he says :*

For one.

Let us pray.   *Collect.*

ALMIGHTY and ever-
lasting God, the
Father of our Lord Jesus
Christ, vouchsafe to look
upon this thy servant N.
(handmaid N.) whom *
[*In supplying ceremonies
add :* of late] thou hast
vouchsafed to call to the
rudiments of the faith :
drive far from *him* all
blindness of heart : break
all the snares of Satan,
wherewith *he* hath been
bound : open to *him,* O
Lord, the gate of thy
mercy, that being filled
with the sign of thy
wisdom, *he* may be set
free from all evil desires,
and may joyfully serve
thee in thy Church, and
prosper from day to day. †
Through the same Christ,
our Lord.   ℟. Amen.

For several.

Let us pray.   *Collect.*

ALMIGHTY and ever-
lasting God, the
Father of our Lord Jesus
Christ, vouchsafe to look
upon these thy servants
N. and N. (handmaids N.
and N.) whom * [*In
supplying   ceremonies
add:*   of   late]   thou
hast vouchsafed to call to
the   rudiments   of   the
faith :   drive   far   from
them   all   blindness   of
heart :   break   all   the
snares of Satan, where-
with *they* have been
bound: open to them, O
Lord, the gate of thy
mercy, that being filled
with the sign of thy
wisdom, they may be set
free from all evil desires,
and may joyfully serve
thee in thy Church, and
prosper from day to day. †
Through the same Christ,
our Lord.   ℟. Amen.

†[*In supplying ceremonies is added :* **that** *he* (**or**
they) may meet to enjoy the grace of thy Baptism,

which *he* has (*or* they have) received, through the partaking of this healing salt.]

6. *Then the Priest blesses salt, which, once blessed, may serve at other times for the same use.*

BLESSING OF THE SALT.

I EXORCISE thee, O creature of salt, in the name of God ✠ the Father almighty, and in the charity of our Lord Jesus ✠ Christ, and in the power of the Holy ✠ Ghost. I exorcise thee through God ✠ the living, through God ✠ the true, through God ✠ the holy, through God ✠, who created thee for the protection of mankind, and commanded thee to be consecrated through his servants for the people that should come to believe ; that in the name of the holy Trinity thou be made a saving sacrament to put to flight the enemy. Therefore we pray thee, O Lord our God, that sanctifying thou wouldest sancti✠fy, and blessing thou wouldest ble✠ss this creature of salt, that it be made to all who receive it perfect healing, abiding in their members, in the name of the same our Lord Jesus Christ, who shall come to judge the living and the dead, and the world by fire. ℞. Amen.

7. *Then he puts a little of the blessed salt into the mouth of the Child, saying (separately to each):*

N. Receive the salt of wisdom : may it be to thee for mercy unto life eternal.

℞. Amen.

Priest : Peace be with thee.
℟. And with thy spirit.

For one.	*For several.*
Let us pray. *Collect.*	Let us pray. *Collect.*
O GOD of our fathers, O God the author of all truth, we humbly entreat thee, that thou wouldest vouchsafe mercifully to look upon this thy servant N. (handmaid N.), and that thou wouldest suffer *him* no longer to hunger, now tasting this (first) [**in suppl. cerem. omit* first] relish of salt, to the end that, being fulfilled with heavenly food, *he* may ever be fervent in spirit, rejoicing in hope, ever serving thy name. † (Lead *him,* O Lord, we beseech thee, to the washing of the new birth, that *he*)	O GOD of our fathers, O God the author of all truth, we humbly entreat thee, that thou wouldest vouchsafe mercifully to look upon these thy servants N. and N. (handmaids N. and N.), and that thou wouldest suffer them no longer to hunger, now tasting this (first) [**in suppl. cerem. omit* first] relish of salt, to the end that, being fulfilled with heavenly food, they may ever be fervent in spirit, rejoicing in hope, ever serving thy name. † (Lead them, O Lord, we beseech thee, to the washing of the new birth, that they)
†[*in suppl. ceremon. substitute :* And we beseech thee, O Lord, that *he* whom thou hast led to the washing of the new birth]	†[*in suppl. ceremon. substitute :* And we beseech thee, O Lord, that they whom thou hast led to the washing of the new birth]

may with thy faithful be worthy to receive the eternal rewards of thy promises. Through Christ, our Lord. ℞. Amen.

may with thy faithful be worthy to receive the eternal rewards of thy promises. Through Christ, our Lord. ℞. Amen.

I EXORCISE thee, unclean spirit, in the name of the Fa✠ther, and of the So✠n, and of the Holy Gho✠st, that thou go out, and depart from this servant (handmaid) of God N. For he himself commands thee, accursed and damned one, who walked with his feet upon the sea, and stretched forth his right hand to Peter as he sank.

I EXORCISE thee, unclean spirit, in the name of the Fa✠ther, and of the So✠n, and of the Holy Gho✠st, that thou go out, and depart from these servants (handmaids) of God (N. and N.) For he himself commands thee, accursed and damned one, who walked with his feet upon the sea, and stretched forth his right hand to Peter as he sank.

THEREFORE, accursed devil, remember thy sentence, and give honour to God the living and the true, give honour to Jesus Christ his Son, and to the Holy Ghost, and depart from this servant (handmaid)

THEREFORE, accursed devil, remember thy sentence, and give honour to God the living and the true, give honour to Jesus Christ his Son, and to the Holy Ghost, and depart from these servants (handmaids) of of God *N.,* forasmuch as our God and Lord Jesus Christ hath vouchsafed to call *him* to his holy grace and benediction, and to the font of Baptism.

God *N.* and *N.,* forasmuch as our God and Lord Jesus Christ hath vouchsafed to call them to his holy grace and benediction, and to the font of Baptism.

8. *Here he signs the Child on the forehead saying (separately to each):*

AND this sign of the holy Cro✠ss, which we set upon *his* brow, do thou, accursed devil, never dare to violate. Through the same Christ, our Lord. ℞. Amen.

9. *Then he lays his hand upon the head of the Child (each Child), and afterwards, holding it extended, says:*

For one.

Let us pray.   *Collect.*

I ENTREAT thy eternal and most just mercy, O Lord holy, Father almighty, everlasting God, author of light and truth, upon this servant (handmaid) of God *N.,* that thou wouldest vouchsafe to enlighten *him* with the light of thine understanding: cleanse *him* and sanctify *him*: give to *him* true

For several.

Let us pray.   *Collect.*

I ENTREAT thy eternal and most just mercy, O Lord holy, Father almighty, everlasting God, author of light and truth, upon these servants (handmaids) of God *N.* and *N.,* that thou wouldest vouchsafe to enlighten them with the light of thine understanding: cleanse and sanctify them: give knowledge, † (that being made worthy of the grace of thy Baptism, *he* may hold firm hope, right counsel and holy doctrine.)

to *them* true knowledge, †(that being made worthy of the grace of thy Baptism, they may hold firm hope, right counsel and holy doctrine.)

---

†[*In suppl. ceremon. substitute :* that *he* may be worthy to enjoy the grace of thy Baptism, which *he* hath received ; that *he* may hold firm hope, right counsel, holy doctrine, that *he* may be meet to keep the grace of thy Baptism.]

† [*In suppl. ceremon. subtute:* that they may be worthy to enjoy the grace of thy Baptism, which they have received; that they may hold firm hope, right counsel, holy doctrine, that they may be meet to keep the grace of thy Baptism.]

Through Christ, our Lord. ℟. Amen.

Through Christ, our Lord. ℟. Amen.

10.   *Then the Priest places the end of his stole which hangs from his left shoulder on the first Child, and leads him (followed by the others) into the Church, saying :*

For one.

N. enter into the temple of God, that thou mayest have part with Christ unto life eternal. ℟. Amen.

For several.

N. AND N., enter into the temple of God, that ye may have part with Christ unto life eternal. ℟. Amen.

IN THE CHURCH.

11. When they are come into the Church, the Priest going towards the Font, says together with the sponsors in a loud voice:

I BELIEVE in God the Father Almighty, Creator of heaven and earth. And in Jesus Christ, his only Son, our Lord : who was conceived by the Holy Ghost ; born of the Virgin Mary ; suffered under Pontius Pilate, was crucified, dead and buried : he descended into hell ; the third day he rose again from the dead ; he ascended into heaven, and sitteth at the right hand of God the Father almighty ; from thence he shall come to judge the living and the dead. I believe in the Holy Ghost ; the Holy Catholic Church ; the Communion of Saints ; the Forgiveness of Sins ; the Resurrection of the Body : and Life Everlasting. Amen.

OUR Father, who art in heaven : hallowed be thy name : thy Kingdom come ; thy will be done on earth as it is in heaven. Give us this day our daily bread : and forgive us our trespasses, as we forgive them that trespass against us. And lead us not into temptation : but deliver us from evil. Amen.

12. And then before he enters the Baptistery, with his back turned to the gate of the screen of the Baptistery, he says:

For one.

I EXORCISE thee, every unclean spirit, in the name of God ✠ the Father almighty, and in the name of Jesus ✠ Christ his Son, our Lord and Judge, and in the power of the Holy ✠ Ghost, that thou depart from this creature of God N. which our Lord hath vouchsafed to call unto his holy temple, *(that it may) [*in suppl. ceremon.:* that it might] become the temple of the living God, and that the Holy Spirit may dwell in it. Through the same Christ, our Lord, who shall come to judge the living and the dead, and the world by fire. ℞. Amen.

For several.

I EXORCISE thee, every unclean spirit, in the name of God ✠ the Father almighty, and in the name of Jesus ✠ Christ his Son, our Lord and Judge, and in the power of the Holy ✠ Ghost, that thou depart from these creatures of God N. and N. which our Lord hath vouchsafed to call unto his holy temple, *(that they may) [*in suppl. ceremon.:* that they might] become the temples of the living God, and that the Holy Spirit may dwell in them. Through the same Christ, our Lord, who shall come to judge the living and the dead, and the world by fire. ℞. Amen.

13. *Then the Priest takes with his thumb of the saliva of his mouth, and touches the ears and nostrils of the Child: and while touching his right and left ears, he says (separately to each):*

B

EPHTHATHA, that is, Be opened. *Then he touches the nostrils, saying:* For an odour of sweetness. And thou, devil, flee away; for the judgment of God draweth nigh.

14. *Then he questions the person to be baptized by name, saying (separately to each):*

N. Dost thou renounce Satan?

The Godfather answers : I do renounce him.

Priest. And all his works?

℞. I do renounce them.

Priest. And all his pomps?

℞. I do renounce them.

15. *Then the Priest dips his thumb in the oil of Catechumens, and anoints the Child on the breast, and between the shoulders in the form of a Cross, saying once (separately to each):*

I ANOINT ✠ thee with the oil of salvation in Christ Jesus our Lord, that thou mayest have eternal life.

℞. Amen.

16. *Then he wipes his thumb and the places anointed with cotton wool, or the like.*

17. *Standing in the same place outside the rails, he lays aside the violet stole, and takes a stole of white colour. Then he enters the Baptistery, which the Godfather also enters with the Child.*

The Priest at the Font questions the person to be baptized (each of those to be baptized) by name, the Godfather answering:

N. **Dost thou believe in God the Father Almighty, Creator of heaven and earth?**

℟. **I do believe.**

Priest. **Dost thou believe in Jesus Christ his only Son, our Lord, who was born into this world, and who suffered for us?**

℟. **I do believe.**

Priest. **Dost thou also believe in the Holy Ghost, the Holy Catholic Church, the Communion of Saints, the Forgiveness of Sins, the Resurrection of the Body, and Life everlasting?**

℟. **I do believe.**

[*In supplying ceremonies: The Priest omits what follows, and resumes the Rite at No. 23, the anointing with Chrism, below, unless that and the remaining Ceremonies had been previously given.*]

18. *Then, naming the person to be baptized, the Priest says (separately to each):*

N. **Wilt thou be baptized?**

The Godfather answers : **I will.**

19. *Then, the Godfather or Godmother, or both (if both be admitted) holding the Child, the Priest takes baptismal water in a vessel or ewer, and pours it thrice on the head of the Child in the form of a Cross, and at the same time uttering the words once*

only, distinctly and with care, says (separately to each) :

N. I baptize thee in the name of the Fa ✠ ther, *he pours the first time,* and of the So ✠ n, *he pours the second time,* and of the Holy ✠ Ghost, *he pours the third time.*

20. *But where the custom of baptizing by immersion exists, the Priest takes the Child, and watching lest it be hurt, carefully immerses it, and baptizes it by trine immersion, and says once only* :

N. I baptize thee in the name of the Fa ✠ ther, and of the So ✠ n, and of the Holy ✠ Ghost.

21. *Then the Godfather or Godmother or both together raise the Child from the sacred Font, receiving it from the hand of the Priest.*

22. *If however there be a doubt whether the Child has been already baptized, he shall use this form* :

N. If thou art not baptized, I baptize thee in the name of the Fa ✠ ther, and of the So ✠ n, and of the Holy ✠ Ghost.

23. *Then he dips his thumb in the sacred Chrism, and anoints the Child on the crown of the head in the form of a Cross, saying (separately to each)* :

ALMIGHTY God, the Father of our Lord Jesus Christ, who hath regenerate thee by water and the Holy Ghost, and hath given unto thee remission

of all thy sins (*here he anoints*); he vouchsafe to anoint ✠ thee with the Chrism of salvation in the same Christ Jesus our Lord unto everlasting life.

℞.   Amen.

The Priest says : Peace be unto thee.

℞.   And with thy spirit.

24.   *Then he wipes his thumb and the place anointed with cotton wool or the like, and puts on the head of the Child a white linen cloth in place of a white vesture saying (separately to each):*

Take this white vesture, and bear it unstained before the judgement seat of our Lord Jesus Christ, that thou mayest be partaker of the life everlasting.

℞.   Amen.

25.   *Then he gives to him, or to the Godfather, a lighted candle, saying (separately to each):*

Take this burning light, and guard thy Baptism without blame ; keep the commandments of God, that when the Lord shall come to the wedding, thou mayest go to meet him with all the Saints in the heavenly court, and live for ever and ever.

℞.   Amen.

26.   *Lastly he says (in the plural for several):*

N. (N. and N.)   Go in peace, and the Lord be with thee (*or* with you).   ℞.   Amen.

27.   *The Rite described above is to be observed also by a Deacon administering solemn Baptism, but*

he must use salt and water previously blessed for this purpose by a Priest.

28. *If several are to be baptized, boys or girls, at the questioning the boys shall be set on the right of the girls; and all things shall be said, as above, in the plural number.*

But all things appointed above to be done and said separately to each *shall be done separately, first to each boy, and then to each girl.*

29. *The Rite given above may be used in England also for adults.*

30. *Before the Child is taken from the Church, or the Godparents depart, the Parish Priest shall accurately enter the names, and other particulars about the Baptism administered, in the Baptismal Book.*

ORDER FOR PRIVATE BAPTISM.

1. *If a child or adult be in danger of death, the Priest, coming to the place where the sick person is, shall baptize him, pouring water thrice or even once upon his head in the form of a Cross, saying*: I baptize thee, etc., *as above, page* 20.

2. *In urgent danger, if there be no Baptismal water to be had, the Priest shall use ordinary water.*

3. *Then, if he has the Chrism, he shall anoint him, and give the white cloth, and lighted candle, as above, page* 21.

ORDER FOR SUPPLYING THE CEREMONIES.

If the person live, all the rites omitted shall be supplied later in the Church. The Order of Baptism given above shall be used, with verbal changes and omissions as there noted [" in supplying of ceremonies "].

BLESSING OF THE FONT OR OF BAPTISMAL WATER

Outside the Vigil of Easter and Pentecost when consecrated water is not to be had.

---

1. *First the Baptismal Font (or vessel) is washed and cleansed, and then filled with clear water. Then the Priest vested in surplice and violet stole, and, if he wish it, also in violet cope, with his Clerks, or even other Priests, the Cross and two candles going before, and the thurible and incense, and with the phials of Chrism and Oil of Catechumens, comes to the Font, and kneeling there, or before the Altar of the Baptistery, says the ordinary Litanies, as below on page* **74.**

2. *Or he may say the shorter Litanies, as in the Missal on Holy Saturday (see also page* **74**).

3. *But before the* ℣. That it may please thee *graciously* to hear us, *he shall stand and say and repeat a second time the following verse*:

That thou wouldest vouchsafe to ble ✠ ss and conse ✠ crate this Font for the regeneration unto thee of new offspring. ℟. We beseech thee, hear us.

Then he shall kneel again and continue the Litanies.

4. *The last* Kyrie, eléison, *having been said, all stand, and the Priest says*: Our Father *and* I believe in God, etc. *(page 16) in a loud voice: which ended he says:*

℣. With thee, O Lord, is the well of life.

℟. And in thy light shall we see light.

℣. O Lord, hear my prayer.

℟. And let my cry come unto thee.

℣. The Lord be with you.

℟. And with thy spirit.

Let us pray.   *Collect.*

ALMIGHTY and everlasting God, be present at the mysteries, be present at the sacraments of thy great goodness : and send forth the spirit of adoption for the regeneration of the new peoples whom the font of Baptism doth bring forth unto thee : that what is to be done by our humble ministry, may be effectually fulfilled by thy power. Through. ℟. Amen.

EXORCISM OF THE WATER.

I EXORCISE thee, O creature of water, by the living ✠ God, by the true ✠ God, by the ho ✠ ly God, by God, who in the beginning through his word divided thee from the dry land : whose Spirit moved upon thee, who commanded thee to flow from paradise.

5. Here he divides the water with his hand, and then scatters it, outside the rim of the Font, towards the four quarters of the world, saying:

And commanded thee to water the whole earth with thy four rivers. Who in the desert by wood bestowed upon thee sweetness when thou wast bitter, that men might drink: who brought thee forth from the rock, that he might refresh the people, wearied with thirst, whom he had delivered out of Egypt. I exorcise thee through Jesus Christ, his only Son, our Lord: who in Cana of Galilee by a wondrous miracle did change thee through his power into wine: who walked upon thee with his feet, and was baptized in thee by John in Jordan. Who brought thee forth together with blood from his side: and commanded his disciples, that they should baptize in thee them that believe, saying: Go ye, teach all nations, baptizing them in the name of the Father, and of the Son, and of the Holy Ghost; that thou mayest be made holy water, blessed water, water that washeth away stains and cleanseth sins. I command thee therefore, every unclean spirit, every phantom, every lie, be rooted out, and flee away from this creature of water; that to them who shall be baptized therein, it may become a font of water springing up unto life eternal, regenerating them unto God the Father, and the Son, and the Holy Ghost, in the name of the same our Lord Jesus Christ, who shall come to judge the living and the dead, and the world by fire. ℟. Amen.

Let us pray. *Collect.*

O LORD holy, Father almighty, everlasting God, who dost sanctify spiritual waters, we humbly entreat thee : that thou wouldest vouchsafe to look upon this ministry of our humble service, and to send forth upon these waters, made ready for the washing and purifying of men, the Angel of holiness ; to the end that, the sins of their former life being washed, and their guilt cleansed, they being regenerate may be worthy to be made a spotless habitation for the Holy Spirit. Through . . . in the unity of the same Holy Spirit.

℞. Amen.

6. *Then he breathes thrice into the water, in three directions according to this figure Ψ: then he puts incense in the thurible, and, having blessed it, censes the Font, with three simple swings. Next, pouring some of the Oil of Catechumens into the water in the form of a Cross, he says in a loud voice :*

May this font be sanctified and made fruitful by the Oil of salvation, for such as shall be born again therefrom unto life eternal, in the name of the Fa ✠ ther, and of the So ✠ n, and of the Holy ✠ Ghost.

℞. Amen.

7. *Then in the same manner, he pours in some of the Chrism, saying :*

May this inpouring of the Chrism of our Lord Jesus Christ, and of the Holy Spirit the Paraclete, be wrought in the name of the holy Trinity.

℞. Amen.

8. *Next he takes both phials of the said holy Oil and the Chrism, and pours in some of both together in the form of a Cross, saying*:

May this commingling of the Chrism of sanctification, and of the Oil of Unction, and of the Water of Baptism be likewise wrought in the name of the Fa ✠ ther, and of the So ✠ n, and of the Ho ✠ ly Ghost. ℞. Amen.

9. *Then, setting down the phials, with his right hand he mingles the holy Oil and the infused Chrism with the Water, and scatters it over the whole Font. Then he wipes his hand with crumbs of bread; and if anyone is to be baptized, he baptizes him, as above. But if none is to be baptized, he shall straightway wash his hands, and the ablution is poured into the sacrarium.*

PUBLICK BAPTISM OF CHILDREN
TO BE USED IN THE CHURCH.
(According to the Book of Common Prayer.)

The Priest coming to the Font, (which is then to be filled with pure Water,) and standing there, shall say:

HATH this child been already baptized, or no?

If they answer No: then shall the Priest proceed as followeth:

DEARLY beloved, forasmuch as all men are conceived and born in sin; and that our Saviour Christ saith, None can enter into the Kingdom of God except he be regenerate and born anew of water and of the Holy Ghost; I beseech you to call upon God the Father, through our Lord Jesus Christ, that of his bounteous mercy he will grant to *this child* that thing which by nature *he* cannot have; that *he* may be baptized with water and the Holy Ghost, and received into Christ's holy Church and made *a lively member* of the same.

Then the Priest shall say:

Let us pray.

ALMIGHTY and everlasting God, who of thy great mercy didst save Noah and his family in the ark from perishing by water; and also didst safely lead the children of Israel, thy people, through the Red Sea, figuring thereby thy holy baptism; and by the baptism of thy well-beloved Son Jesus Christ, in the river Jordan, didst sanctify Water to the mystical

washing away of sin; we beseech thee, for thine
infinite mercies, that thou wilt mercifully look upon
this Child; wash *him* and sanctify *him* with the Holy
Ghost; that *he*, being delivered from thy wrath, may
be received into the ark of Christ's Church and, being
steadfast in faith, joyful through hope, and rooted in
charity, may so pass the waves of this troublesome
world, that finally *he* may come to the land of everlasting life, there to reign with thee, world without end.
Through Jesus Christ, our Lord. *Amen.*

Let us pray.

A LMIGHTY and immortal God, the aid of all that
need; the helper of all that flee to thee for
succour; the life of them that believe; and the
resurrection of the dead; we call upon thee for *this
Infant* that *he*, coming to thy holy Baptism, may
receive remission of *his* sins by spiritual regeneration.
Receive *him*, O Lord, as thou hast promised by thy
well-beloved Son, saying: Ask, and ye shall have;
seek, and ye shall find; knock, and it shall be opened
unto you; so give now unto us that ask; let us that
seek, find; open the gate unto us that knock; that
this Infant may enjoy the everlasting benediction of
thy heavenly washing, and may come to the eternal
kingdom which thou hast promised by Christ our
Lord. *Amen.*

*Then shall the people stand up, and the Priest
shall say:*

H EAR the words of the Gospel, written by Saint
Mark, in the tenth chapter, at the thirteenth verse.

T HEY brought young children to Christ, that he
should touch them; and his disciples rebuked those
that brought them. But when Jesus saw it, he was

much displeased, and said unto them, Suffer the little children to come unto me, and forbid them not; for of such is the kingdom of God. Verily I say unto you, Whosoever shall not receive the kingdom of God as a little child, he shall not enter therein. And he took them up in his arms, put his hands upon them, and blessed them.

After the Gospel is read, the Minister shall make this brief exhortation upon the words of the Gospel:

BELOVED, ye hear in this Gospel the words of our Saviour Christ, that he commanded the children to be brought unto him; how he blamed those that would have kept them from him; how he exhorteth all men to follow their innocency. Ye perceive how by his outward gesture and deed he declared his good will towards them; for he embraced them in his arms, he laid his hands upon them, and blessed them. Doubt ye not therefore, but earnestly believe, that he will likewise favourably receive *this* present *Infant*; that he will embrace *him* with the arms of his mercy; that he will give unto *him* the blessing of eternal life, and make *him partaker* of his everlasting kingdom. Wherefore we being thus persuaded of the good will of our heavenly Father towards *this Infant*, declared by his Son Jesus Christ; and nothing doubting but that he favourably alloweth this charitable work of ours in bringing *this Infant* to his holy Baptism; let us faithfully and devoutly give thanks unto him, and say:

ALMIGHTY and everlasting God, heavenly Father, we give thee humble thanks for that thou hast vouchsafed to call us to the knowledge of thy grace, and faith in thee: increase this knowledge and con-

firm this faith in us evermore: Give thy Holy Spirit
to *this Infant* that *he* may be born again, and made
an heir of everlasting salvation; through our Lord
Jesus Christ, who liveth and reigneth with thee and
the holy Spirit, now and for ever. *Amen.*

*Then shall the Priest speak unto the Godfathers
and Godmothers on this wise:*

DEARLY beloved, ye have brought this Child here
to be baptized; ye have prayed that our Lord
Jesus Christ would vouchsafe to receive *him*, to
release *him* of *his* sins, to sanctify *him* with the Holy
Ghost, to give *him* the kingdom of heaven, and everlasting life. Ye have heard also that our Lord Jesus
Christ hath promised in his Gospel to grant all these
things that ye have prayed for: which promise he,
for his part, will most surely keep and perform.
Wherefore, after this promise made by Christ, *this
Infant* must also faithfully, for *his* part, promise by
you that are *his* sureties, until *he* come of age to take
it upon *himself*, that *he* will renounce the devil and
all his works, and constantly believe God's holy word,
and obediently keep his commandments.

I demand therefore,

DOST thou, in the name of this Child, renounce the
devil and all his works, the vain pomp and glory of
the world, with all the covetous desires of the same,
and the carnal desires of the flesh, so that thou wilt
not follow, nor be led by them?

Answer. I renounce them all.

Minister.

DOST thou believe in God the Father Almighty,
Maker of heaven and earth?

And in Jesus Christ his only-begotten Son our
Lord? And that he was conceived by the Holy Ghost;

born of the Virgin Mary; suffered under Pontius
Pilate, was crucified, dead, and buried; that he went
down into hell, and also did rise again the third day;
that he ascended into heaven and sitteth at the
right hand of God the Father Almighty; and from
thence shall come again at the end of the world, to
judge the quick and the dead?

And dost thou believe in the Holy Ghost; the
Holy Catholic Church; the Communion of Saints;
the Remission of sins; the Resurrection of the flesh;
and everlasting life after death?

Answer. All this I steadfastly believe.

Minister:

Wilt thou be baptized in this faith?

Answer. That is my desire.

Minister:

Wilt thou then obediently keep God's holy will
and commandments, and walk in the same all the
days of thy life?

Answer. I will.

Then shall the Priest say:

O MERCIFUL God, grant that the old Adam in
this Child may be so buried, that the new man
may be raised up in *him. Amen.*

GRANT that all carnal affections may die in *him,*
and that all things belonging to the Spirit may live
and grow in *him. Amen.*

GRANT that *he* may have power and strength to
have victory, and to triumph, against the devil, the
world, and the flesh. *Amen.*

c

GRANT that whosoever is here dedicated to thee by our office and ministry may also be endued with heavenly virtues, and everlastingly rewarded, through thy mercy, O blessed Lord God, who dost live and govern all things, world without end. *Amen.*

ALMIGHTY, everliving God, whose most dearly beloved Son, Jesus Christ, for the forgiveness of sins, did shed out of his most precious side both water and blood; and gave commandment to his disciples that they should go teach all nations, and baptize them, in the name of the Father, and of the Son, and of the Holy Ghost; Regard we beseech thee, the supplications of thy congregation; sanctify this water to the mystical washing away of sin; and grant that *this Child*, now to be baptized therein, may receive the fulness of thy grace, and ever remain in the number of thy faithful and elect children; through Jesus Christ our Lord. *Amen.*

Then the Priest shall take the Child into his hands and say to the Godfathers and Godmothers:

Name this Child.

And then, naming it after them he shall (if they certify that the Child may well endure it) dip it in the Water discreetly and warily saying:

N . . . , I baptize thee In the name of the Father, and of the Son, and of the Holy Ghost. Amen.

[But if they certify that the Child is weak, it shall suffice to pour Water upon it, saying the fore-said words:

N . . . , I baptize thee In the name of the Father, and of the Son, and of the Holy Ghost. Amen.]

Then shall the Priest say:

WE receive this Child into the congregation of
Christ's flock, *and do sign *him* with the sign of
* *Here the Priest* the Cross, in token that hereafter *he*
shall make a Cross shall not be ashamed to confess the
upon the Child's
forehead. faith of Christ crucified, and manfully
to fight under his banner, against sin, the world, and
the devil; and to continue Christ's faithful soldier and
servant unto *his* life's end.   Amen.

[*For the ancient Ceremonies, see pages* 20-21, *Nos.* 23-25.]

Then shall the Priest say:

SEEING now, dearly beloved brethren, that *this*
Child is regenerate and grafted into the body of
Christ's Church, let us give thanks unto Almighty
God for these benefits; and with one accord make our
prayers unto him, that *this* Child may lead the rest
of *his life* according to this beginning.

Then shall be said, all kneeling:

OUR Father, which art in heaven, Hallowed be thy
Name. Thy kingdom come. Thy will be done, in
earth as it is in heaven. Give us this day our daily
bread. And forgive us our trespasses, As we forgive
them that trespass against us. And lead us not into
temptation; But deliver us from evil. Amen.

Then shall the Priest say:

WE yield thee hearty thanks, most merciful Father,
that it hath pleased thee to regenerate *this*
Infant with thy Holy Spirit, to receive *him* for thine
own *Child* by adoption, and to incorporate *him* into
thy holy Church. And humbly we beseech thee to
grant that *he* being dead unto sin, and living unto

righteousness, and being buried with Christ in his death, may crucify the old man, and utterly abolish the whole body of sin; and that as *he* is made *partaker* of the death of thy Son, *he* may also be *partaker* of his resurrection; so that finally, with the residue of thy holy Church, *he* may be *an inheritor* of thine ever-lasting kingdom; through Christ our Lord. *Amen.*

Then, all standing up, the Priest shall say to the Godfathers and Godmothers this Exhortation following:

FORASMUCH as *this Child* hath promised by you *his* sureties to renounce the devil and all his works, to believe in God and to serve him; ye must remember that it is your parts and duties to see that *this Infant* be taught, so soon as *he* shall be able to learn, what a solemn vow, promise, and profession *he hath* here made by you. And that *he* may know these things the better, ye shall call upon *him* to hear sermons; and chiefly ye shall provide that *he* may learn the Creed, the Lord's Prayer, and the Ten Commandments, in the vulgar tongue, and all other things which a Christian ought to know and believe to his soul's health; and that *this child* may be virtuously brought up to lead a godly and christian life; remembering always that Baptism doth represent unto us our profession; which is, to follow the example of our Saviour Christ, and to be made like unto him; that, as he died and rose again for us, so should we, who are baptized, die from sin, and rise again unto righteousness, continually mortifying all our evil and corrupt affections, and daily proceeding in all virtue and godliness of living.

Then shall he add and say:

Ye are to take care that *this Child* be brought to the Bishop, to be confirmed by him, so soon as *he* can say the Creed, the Lord's Prayer, and the Ten Commandments, in the vulgar tongue, and be further instructed in the Church-Catechism set forth for that purpose.

It is certain by God's word that Children which are baptized, dying before they commit actual sin, are undoubtedly saved.

PRIVATE BAPTISM OF CHILDREN
IN HOUSES.

The Curates of every Parish shall often admonish the people, that they defer not the Baptism of their Children longer than the first or second Sunday next after their birth, or other Holy-day falling between, unless upon a great and reasonable cause, to be approved by the Curate.

And also they shall warn them, that without like great cause and necessity they procure not their Children to be baptized at home in their houses. But when need shall compel them so to do, then Baptism shall be administered on this fashion:

First, let the Minister of the Parish (or, in his absence, any other lawful Minister that can be procured) with them that are present call upon God, and say the Lord's Prayer, and so many of the Collects appointed to be said before in the Form of Publick Baptism, as the time and present exigence will suffer. And then, the Child being named by some one that is present, the Minister shall pour Water upon it, saying these words:

N. I baptize thee in the Name of the Father, and of the Son, and of the Holy Ghost. Amen.

Then, all kneeling down, the Minister shall give thanks unto God, and say:

WE yield thee hearty thanks, most merciful Father, that it hath pleased thee to regenerate *this Infant* with thy holy Spirit, to receive *him* for thine own *Child* by adoption, and to incorporate *him* into thy holy Church. And we humbly beseech thee to grant, that as *he* is now made *partaker* of the death of thy Son, so *he* may be also of his resurrection; and that finally, with the residue of thy Saints, *he* may inherit thine everlasting kingdom; through the same thy Son Jesus Christ our Lord. *Amen.*

And let them not doubt, but that the Child so baptized is lawfully and sufficiently baptized, and ought not to be baptized again. Yet nevertheless, if the Child, which is after this sort baptized, do afterward live, it is expedient that it be brought into the Church, to the intent that, if the Minister of the same Parish did himself baptize that Child, the Congregation may be certified of the true Form of Baptism, by him privately before used: In which case he shall say thus:

I CERTIFY you, that according to the due and prescribed Order of the Church, *at such a time,* and *at such a place,* before divers witnesses I baptized this Child.

But if the Child were baptized by any other lawful Minister, then the Minister of the Parish, where the Child was born or christened, shall examine and try whether the Child be lawfully baptized, or no. In which case, if those that bring any Child to the Church do answer, that the same Child is already baptized, then shall the Minister examine them further, saying:

BY whom was this Child baptized?
Who was present when this Child was baptized?

Because some things essential to this Sacrament may happen to be omitted through fear or haste, in such times of extremity; therefore I demand further of you,

With what matter was this Child baptized?

With what words was this Child baptized?

And if the Minister shall find by the answers of such as bring the Child, that all things were done as they ought to be; then shall not he christen the Child again, but shall receive him as one of the flock of true christian people, saying thus:

I CERTIFY you, that in this case all is well done, and according unto due order, concerning the baptizing of this Child; who being born in original sin, and in the wrath of God, is now, by the laver of Regeneration in Baptism, received into the number of the children of God, and heirs of everlasting life: for our Lord Jesus Christ doth not deny his grace and mercy unto such Infants, but most lovingly doth call them unto him, as the holy Gospel doth witness to our comfort on this wise.

St. *Mark* x. 13.

THEY brought young children to Christ, that he should touch them; and his disciples rebuked those that brought them. But when Jesus saw it, he was much displeased, and said unto them, Suffer the little children to come unto me, and forbid them not; for of such is the kingdom of God. Verily, I say unto you, Whosoever shall not receive the kingdom of God as a little child, he shall not enter therein. And he took them up in his arms, put his hands upon them, and blessed them.

After the Gospel is read, the Minister shall make this brief Exhortation upon the words of the Gospel.

BELOVED, ye hear in this Gospel the words of our Saviour Christ, that he commanded the children to be brought unto him; how he blamed those that

would have kept them from him; how he exhorted all
men to follow their innocency. Ye perceive how by
his outward gesture and deed he declared his good
will toward them; for he embraced them in his arms,
he laid his hands upon them, and blessed them.
Doubt ye not therefore, but earnestly believe, that
he hath likewise favourably received *this* present
Infant; that he hath embraced *him* with the arms
of his mercy; and (as he hath promised in his holy
Word) will give unto *him* the blessing of eternal life,
and made *him partaker* of his everlasting kingdom.
Wherefore, we being thus persuaded of the good will
of our heavenly Father, declared by his Son Jesus
Christ towards *this Infant*, let us faithfully and
devoutly give thanks unto him, and say the Prayer
which the Lord himself taught us :

OUR Father, which art in heaven, Hallowed be
thy Name. Thy kingdom come. Thy will be
done, in earth as it is in heaven. Give us this day
our daily bread. And forgive us our trespasses, As
we forgive them that trespass against us. And lead
us not into temptation; But deliver us from evil.
Amen.

ALMIGHTY and everlasting God, heavenly Father,
we give thee humble thanks, that thou hast
vouchsafed to call us to the knowledge of thy grace,
and faith in thee; Increase this knowledge, and confirm this faith in us evermore. Give thy holy Spirit
to *this Infant*, that *he*, being born again, and being
made *an heir* of everlasting salvation, through our
Lord Jesus Christ, may continue thy *servant*, and
attain thy promise; through the same our Lord Jesus
Christ thy Son, who liveth and reigneth with thee
and the Holy Spirit, now and for ever. *Amen.*

Then shall the Priest demand the Name of the Child; which being by the Godfathers and Godmothers pronounced, the Minister shall say:

DOST thou, in the name of this Child, renounce the devil and all his works, the vain pomp and glory of this world, with all covetous desires of the same, and the carnal desires of the flesh, so that thou wilt not follow, nor be led by them?

Answer. I renounce them all.

Minister:

DOST thou believe in God the Father Almighty, Maker of heaven and earth?

And in Jesus Christ his only-begotten Son our Lord? And that he was conceived by the Holy Ghost; born of the Virgin Mary; that he suffered under Pontius Pilate, was crucified, dead, and buried; that he went down into hell, and also did rise again the third day; that he ascended into heaven, and sitteth at the right hand of God the Father Almighty; and from thence shall come again at the end of the world, to judge the quick and the dead?

And dost thou believe in the Holy Ghost; the holy Catholick Church; the Communion of Saints; the Remission of sins; the Resurrection of the flesh; and everlasting life after death?

Answer. All this I stedfastly believe.

Minister:

WILT thou then obediently keep God's holy will and commandments, and walk in the same all the days of thy life?

Answer. I will.

Then the Priest shall say:

WE receive this Child into the congregation of Christ's flock, *and do sign *him* with the sign of the Cross, in token that hereafter *he* shall not be ashamed to confess the faith of Christ crucified, and manfully to fight under his banner, against sin, the world, and the devil; and to continue Christ's faithful soldier and servant unto *his* life's end. Amen.

* *Here the Priest shall make a Cross upon the Child's forehead.*

[*For ancient Ceremonies, see page* 20.]

Then the Priest shall say:

SEEING now, dearly beloved brethren, that *this Child is* by Baptism regenerate, and grafted into the body of Christ's Church, let us give thanks unto Almighty God for these benefits; and with one accord make our prayers unto him, that *he* may lead the rest of *his* life according to this beginning.

Then the Priest shall say:

WE yield thee most hearty thanks, most merciful Father, that it hath pleased thee to regenerate *this Infant* with thy holy Spirit, to receive *him* for thine own *Child* by adoption, and to incorporate *him* into thy holy Church. And humbly we beseech thee to grant, that *he* being dead unto sin, and living unto righteousness, and being buried with Christ in his death, may crucify the old man, and utterly abolish the whole body of sin; and that, as he is made *partaker* of the death of thy Son, *he* may also be *partaker* of his resurrection; so that finally, with the residue of thy holy Church; *he* may be *an inheritor* of thine everlasting kingdom; through Jesus Christ our Lord. *Amen.*

Then, all standing up, the Minister shall make this Exhortation to the Godfathers and Godmothers.

FORASMUCH as *this Child hath* promised by you *his* sureties to renounce the devil and all his works, to believe in God, and to serve him; ye must remember, that it is your parts and duties to see that *this Infant* be taught, so soon as *he* shall be able to learn, what a solemn vow, promise, and profession *he hath* made by you. And that *he* may know these things the better, ye shall call upon *him* to hear Sermons; and chiefly ye shall provide, that *he* may learn the Creed, the Lord's Prayer, and the Ten Commandments, in the vulgar tongue, and all other things which a Christian ought to know and believe to his soul's health; and that *this Child* may be virtuously brought up to lead a godly and a christian life; remembering alway, that Baptism doth represent unto us our profession; which is, to follow the example of our Saviour Christ, and to be made like unto him; that, as he died, and rose again for us, so should we, who are baptized, die from sin, and rise again unto righteousness; continually mortifying all our evil and corrupt affections, and daily proceeding in all virtue and godliness of living.

But if they which bring the Infant to the Church do make such uncertain answers to the Priest's questions, as that it cannot appear that the Child was baptized with Water, In the Name of the Father, and of the Son, and of the Holy Ghost, (which are essential parts of Baptism,) then let the Priest baptize it in the form before appointed for Publick Baptism of Infants; saving that at the dipping of the Child in the Font, he shall use this form of words:

IF thou art not already baptized, *N.* I baptize thee In the Name of the Father, and of the Son, and of the Holy Ghost. Amen.

THE SACRAMENT OF PENANCE

The penitent, on kneeling before the Priest, at once says:

Father, give me your blessing for I have sinned; *and the Priest forthwith gives*

THE BLESSING.

THE Lord be in thy heart and upon thy lips, that thou mayest meetly and rightly confess thy sins, in the name of the Father, and of the ✠ Son, and of the Holy Ghost.   Amen.

The penitent then enumerates his sins and, if desired, the Priest will give him counsel and advice, and before pronouncing absolution he shall impose a penance.

It is desirable when there are many to be confessed, that the faithful should be taught to say the whole of the preparatory form immediately before approaching the confessional, and then, as soon as the Priest has given the customary blessing, straightway to commence, and say:

Since my last confession, which . . . ago, I have sinned, etc.

When the Priest wishes to absolve a penitent, after a penance enjoined and accepted, he shall say:

ALMIGHTY God have mercy upon thee, forgive thee thy sins, and bring thee to everlasting life. ℞. Amen.

2. Then raising his right hand toward the penitent, he says:

The almighty and merciful Lord grant unto thee pardon, ✠ absolution, and remission of thy sins. Amen.

OUR LORD Jesus Christ absolve thee; and I by his authority absolve thee from every bond of excommunication (suspension) and interdict, so far as I have power, and thou hast need. Furthermore I absolve thee from thy sins, in the name of the Father, and of the ✠ Son, and of the Holy Ghost. Amen.

[*Form from the B.C.P.*]

OUR LORD Jesus Christ, who hath left power to his Church to absolve all sinners who truly repent and believe in him, of his great mercy forgive thee thine offences; And by his authority committed to me, I absolve thee from all thy sins; in the name of the Father, and of the ✠ Son, and of the Holy Ghost. Amen.

---

3. If the penitent be a laic, the word suspension *is omitted. A Bishop in absolving the faithful makes the sign of the Cross thrice.*

THE PASSION of our Lord Jesus Christ, the merits of the Blessed Virgin Mary and of all the Saints, whatsoever good thou hast done or evil thou hast endured, be to thee for remission of sins, increase of grace, and the reward of eternal life. Amen.

4. *For reasonable cause the prayers given above may be omitted, and only the Absolution,* **Our Lord Jesus Christ,** *etc., need be said.*

5. *When grave necessity presses in danger of death, the Priest may say briefly:*

I ABSOLVE thee from all censures and sins, in the name of the Father, and of the ✠ Son, and of the Holy Ghost. Amen.

THE ORDER OF HOLY COMMUNION

Two candles having been lit upon the altar; and the Priest having washed his hands and vested in a surplice and stole (either the colour of the day, or white—violet instead of black on All Souls' Day), with hands joined, unless carrying the burse, and preceded by the Clerk, goes to the Altar.

He genuflects upon the pavement, then going up to the Altar spreads the corporal; opens the tabernacle; again genuflects; takes out the pyx and places it upon the corporal, and again genuflects. The Clerk kneeling makes the general Confession saying:

I CONFESS to God almighty, to blessed Mary ever Virgin, to blessed Michael the Archangel, to blessed John the Baptist, to the holy Apostles Peter and Paul, to all the Saints, and to thee, Father, that I have sinned exceedingly in thought, word and deed, through my fault, my own fault, my own most grievous fault. Therefore I beg blessed Mary ever Virgin, blessed Michael the Archangel, blessed John the Baptist, the holy Apostles Peter and Paul, all the Saints, and thee, Father, to pray for me to the Lord our God.

2. The Priest genuflects again, turns to the people (taking care not to turn his back upon the Sacrament,) and says at the Gospel corner:

ALMIGHTY God have mercy upon you, forgive you your sins, and bring you to everlasting life. ℟. Amen.

THE ALMIGHTY and merciful Lord grant unto you pardon, ✠ absolution, and remission of your sins. ℟. Amen.

3. *Then turning to the Altar, he genuflects and takes the pyx with his left hand; and holding the Sacrament with his right hand, elevates it above the pyx. He then turns himself towards the people in the midst of the Altar, and without making the sign of the Cross says once only:*

BEHOLD the Lamb of God, behold him that taketh away the sins of the world.

And then these words, repeating them thrice:

LORD, I am not worthy that thou shouldest come under my roof, but speak the word only and my soul shall be healed.

4. *Afterwards the Priest proceeds to communicate the people, beginning at the Epistle side of the Altar; but if there be other Priests or Clerics to be communicated, he shall begin with them, and they shall kneel on the Altar step. Priests and Deacons in receiving holy Communion wear a stole, which may be of the same colour as the Celebrant's or white.*

5. *The Priest in delivering the Sacrament, makes the sign of the Cross with it over the pyx, saying:*

THE BODY of our Lord Jesus Christ preserve thy soul unto everlasting life. Amen.

6. *When all have communicated, the Priest returns to the Altar; places the pyx on it; genuflects, and says:*

O SACRED banquet, wherein Christ is received, the memory of his Passion renewed, the mind is filled with grace, and a pledge of future glory given unto us. (*Adding in Eastertide and through the Octave of Corpus Christi* **Alleluia.**)

7.   ℣. THOU gavest them bread from heaven.
                                       (Alleluia.)

℞.   Containing in itself all sweetness.
                                       (Alleluia.)

℣.   O Lord hear my prayer.
℞.   And let my cry come unto thee.
℣.   The Lord be with you.
℞.   And with thy spirit.

Let us pray.   *Collect.*

O GOD, who under a wonderful Sacrament hast left unto us a memorial of thy passion: grant us, we beseech thee, so to venerate the sacred mysteries of thy Body and Blood; that we may ever perceive within ourselves the fruit of thy redemption. Who livest and reignest with God the Father, in the unity of the Holy Ghost, one God, world without end. ℞. Amen.

In Eastertide the following Collect is said instead of the preceding:

P OUR forth upon us, O Lord, the Spirit of thy charity: that as thou hast fulfilled us with these paschal sacraments ; so, of thy goodness, thou wouldest make us to be of one heart and mind. Through Jesus Christ thy Son, our Lord: Who liveth and reigneth with thee in the unity of the

same Holy Spirit, ever one God, world without end.
℞. Amen.

8. *Before the Priest replaces the Sacrament,*
he cleanses his fingers in a vessel of water prepared
for that purpose, and wipes them on a purificator: and
the water of the ablution is cast into the piscina at a
convenient time. He then replaces the pyx in the
tabernacle, genuflects again, and locks the door of the
tabernacle.

9. *Then raising his eyes to heaven, extending,*
elevating, and joining his hands, and bowing his head
to the Cross, the Priest says:

THE blessing of God almighty, *And turning to*
the people, blessing them once only, he proceeds:
the Father, the S✠on, and the Holy Ghost, descend
upon you, and remain with you alway. ℞. Amen.

10. *If Holy Communion is given from the taber-*
nacle immediately before or after a Mass of Requiem,
while the Priest is vested in black, the foregoing
blessing shall be omitted.

11. *If in case of necessity, a Deacon gives Holy*
Communion, the foregoing rite is observed, and the
Deacon shall give the blessing as above.

12. *If a Bishop administers the Holy Com-*
munion, he uses the above rite, but gives the blessing
in the episcopal form and manner.

THE COMMUNION OF THE SICK

When a sick person is to be communicated, the following shall be prepared in his room :

A table covered with a fair linen cloth, having upon it two candles, or at least one; a crucifix; and other suitable adornments.

A vessel and water, with a purificator for the ablution of the Priest's fingers.

A houseling cloth, unless a communion paten is to be used.

A vessel of holy Water and sprinkler, unless the Priest bring them with him.

2. *The Priest who carries the Holy Sacrament should be vested in surplice, white stole, and humeral veil, and should be accompanied by a Clerk or some other devout person bearing a light and a bell.*

Upon the way to the house the Priest will recite **PSALM** 51, *and other of the Penitential Psalms.*

On entering the sick man's room the Priest says :

℣. **Peace be to this house.**

℟. **And to all that dwell in it.**

3. *Placing the pyx upon the table, on an unfolded corporal, he genuflects and worships. And all present shall likewise kneel and adore.*

The humeral veil is then laid aside and the Priest, if not already vested, puts on a surplice and white stole.

Next he takes the vessel of holy Water and sprinkles the sick person and the room wherein he lieth, saying:

Ant. Thou shalt purge me, O Lord, with hyssop, and I shall be clean; thou shalt wash me, and I shall be whiter than snow.

Psalm 51.　Have mercy upon me, O God, after thy great goodness.

Glory be.　As it was.

Ant. Thou shalt purge me, etc.

℣. Our help is in the name of the Lord.

℟. Who hath made heaven and earth.

℣. O Lord, hear my prayer.

℟. And let my cry come unto thee.

℣. The Lord be with you.

℟. And with thy spirit.

Let us pray.　　　　　　　　　　　*Collect.*

GRACIOUSLY hear us, O Lord holy, Father almighty, everlasting God: and vouchsafe to send thy holy Angel from heaven, to guard and cherish, protect, visit and defend all who dwell in this dwelling-place.　Through Christ, our Lord. ℟. Amen.

4. This done, he approaches the sick person, that he may learn whether he be well disposed to receive the Holy Sacrament, and whether he wishes to confess any sins; and he shall hear his confession and absolve him. But the sick man ought to have confessed previously, unless the circumstances have prevented him from doing so.

5. *Then, the general confession being made as usual (see pp. 48 or 59) either by the sick man, or in his name by another, the Priest says in the singular (or plural), if there be several):*

A LMIGHTY God, etc., The almighty, etc.

6. *After which the Priest genuflects, takes the Sacrament from the pyx, and raising it shews it to the sick person, saying:*

B EHOLD the Lamb of God : behold him that taketh away the sins of the world.

And in the accustomed manner says three times:

Lord, I am not worthy that thou shouldest come under my roof, but speak the word only and my soul shall be healed.

9. *And the sick person shall say the same words with the Priest once at least, in a low voice.*

Then the Priest gives the Eucharist to the sick person (if by way of Viaticum with these words):

R ECEIVE brother (sister) the Viaticum of the Body of our Lord Jesus Christ, and may he preserve thee from the malicious enemy and bring thee to everlasting life. Amen.

10. *If not by way of Viaticum then with these words:*

T HE Body of our Lord Jesus Christ preserve thy soul unto everlasting life. Amen.

11. *The Priest washes his fingers and afterwards proceeds:*

℣. The Lord be with you.

℟ And with thy spirit.

Let us pray.   *Collect.*

O LORD holy, Father almighty, everlasting God, we faithfully beseech thee that the most sacred Body of our Lord Jesus Christ thy Son, which our *brother* hath received, may avail for the everlasting healing both of body and soul : Who liveth and reigneth with thee in the unity of the Holy Ghost, ever one God, world without end. ℟. Amen.

12.   Then in silence, the blessing is given by making, with the pyx or ciborium, the sign of the cross; but if the pyx or ciborium be now empty, the blessing is given verbally, as usual.

THE BLESSING of God almighty, the Father, the ✠ Son, and the Holy Ghost, descend upon thee, and remain with thee alway.   Amen.

In the former case the priest shall return to the church with the Sacrament in the same manner as he came to the house, but upon the way instead of Penitential Psalms, he shall repeat PSALM 148 *and other psalms of praise.*

13.   When the priest has placed the Sacrament upon the Altar, he genuflects and then says:

℣. **Thou gavest them bread from heaven.** (*In Eastertide and through the Octave of Corpus Christi* : **Alleluia.**)

℟. **Containing in itself all sweetness. (Alleluia.)**

℣. The Lord be with you.

℟ And with thy spirit.

Let us pray. *Collect.*

O GOD, who under a wonderful Sacrament hast
left us a memorial of thy Passion : grant us,
we beseech thee so to venerate the sacred
mysteries of thy Body and Blood that we may ever
perceive within ourselves the fruit of thy
redemption : Who livest and reignest, world
without end. ℟. Amen.

14. *And before replacing the pyx in the taber-*
nacle the Priest shall bless the people therewith,
saying nothing.

15. *If, in a case of necessity, Holy Communion*
be administered by a Deacon, he follows the foregoing
rite in all respects, and gives the Blessing.

16. *Those sick persons who have been confined to*
their beds for one month, and who have no substantial
grounds for expecting a speedy recovery may, if this is
in accord with the prudent advice of their confessor,
receive Holy Communion once or twice a week without
strictly fasting, that is, after having taken a small
quantity of liquid nourishment or (even solid)
medicine.

17. *When the sick person is a Priest or Deacon*
he should be vested for Communion in a surplice and
white stole : or in stole only if his condition renders it
at all inconvenient to vest him in a surplice.

18. *If at the time of administering the Viaticum*
it be doubtful whether the sick person is physically

able to swallow, a little plain water or wine may be given with, or immediately before or directly after, Communion. In some cases it may be desirable to communicate with only a small portion of the Host.

19. In the event of unintentional irreverence through coughing or otherwise, the houseling cloth with any Particles thereon, may be either buried or burned.

20. The ablution of the Priest's fingers may be disposed of, either by giving to the sick person, if he be able to take it, or else it may be cast into the fire, or taken back to the church and placed in the piscina.

CONCERNING THE COMMUNION OF THE SICK.

(1) By Canon Law Mass may only be celebrated outside a Church or Oratory with the permission of the Ordinary, which may only be given for a grave and just cause, and not habitually.

(2) In grave emergency a Priest may celebrate Mass, even not fasting or a second time in the day, in order to give Holy Communion to the dying, if the Reserved Sacrament may not be had. If this should occur on Good Friday, he should celebrate a Votive Mass of the Passion.

Such procedure should rarely be necessary, as by Canon Law the Blessed Sacrament must be reserved in every Cathedral and Parish Church.

It will therefore seldom happen that the Priest celebrates in a sick man's room, as the following Order provides. But the portions of this Order not enclosed in brackets will be of use to those who, in administering the Reserved Sacrament, employ forms of words contained in the Book of Common Prayer.

THE COMMUNION OF THE SICK

(ACCORDING TO THE ORDER OF THE BOOK OF COMMON PRAYER.)

[*The Curate shall celebrate the holy Communion in the sick man's house, beginning with the Collect, Epistle, and Gospel, here following.*

THE COLLECT.

ALMIGHTY, everliving God, Maker of mankind, who dost correct those whom thou dost love, and chastise every one whom thou dost receive; We beseech thee to have mercy upon this thy servant visited with thine hand, and to grant that *he* may take *his* sickness patiently, and recover *his* bodily health, (if it be thy gracious will;) and whensoever *his* soul shall depart from the body, it may be without spot presented unto thee; through Jesus Christ our Lord. *Amen.*

THE EPISTLE. Hebrews 12.5.

MY son, despise not thou the chastening of the Lord, nor faint when thou art rebuked of him. For whom the Lord loveth he chasteneth; and scourgeth every son whom he receiveth.

THE GOSPEL. St. John 5.24.

VERILY, verily, I say unto you, He that heareth my word, and believeth on him that sent me, hath everlasting life, and shall not come into condemnation; but is passed from death unto life.]

After which the Priest shall proceed according to the form before prescribed for the holy Communion, beginning at these words:

YE that do truly and earnestly repent you of your sins, and are in love and charity with your neighbours, and intend to lead a new life, following the commandments of God, and walking from henceforth in his holy ways; Draw near with faith, and take this holy Sacrament to your comfort; and make your humble confession to Almighty God, meekly kneeling upon your knees.

Then shall this general Confession be made, in the name of all those that are minded to receive the holy Communion, by one of the Ministers; both he and all the people kneeling humbly upon their knees, and saying:

ALMIGHTY God, Father of our Lord Jesus Christ, Maker of all things, Judge of all men; We acknowledge and bewail our manifold sins and wickedness, Which we, from time to time, most grievously have committed, By thought, word, and deed, Against thy Divine Majesty, Provoking most justly thy wrath and indignation against us. We do earnestly repent, And are heartily sorry for these our misdoings; The remembrance of them is grievous unto us; the burden of them is intolerable. Have mercy upon us, Have mercy upon us, most merciful Father; For thy Son our Lord Jesus Christ's sake, Forgive us all that is past; And grant that we may ever hereafter Serve and please thee In newness of life, To the honour and glory of thy Name; Through Jesus Christ our Lord. Amen.

Then shall the Priest stand up, and turning himself to the people, pronounce this Absolution:

ALMIGHTY God, our heavenly Father, who of his great mercy hath promised forgiveness of sins to all them that with hearty repentence and true faith turn unto him; Have mercy upon you; pardon and deliver you from all your sins; confirm and strengthen you in all goodness; and bring you to everlasting life; through Jesus Christ our Lord. *Amen.*

Then shall the Priest say:

Hear what comfortable words our Saviour Christ saith unto all that truly turn to him.

COME unto me all that travail and are heavy laden, and I will refresh you. *St. Matthew* 11.28.

So God loved the world, that he gave his only-begotten Son, to the end that all that believe in him should not perish but have everlasting life. *St. John* 3.16.

Hear also what Saint Paul saith.

This is a true saying, and worthy of all men to be received, That Christ Jesus came into the world to save sinners. 1 *Timothy* 1.15.

Hear also what Saint John saith.

If any man sin, we have an Advocate with the Father, Jesus Christ the righteous; and he is the propitiation for our sins. 1 *St. John* 2.1.

[*After which the Priest shall proceed, saying:*

Lift up your hearts.

Answer. We lift them up unto the Lord.

Priest. Let us give thanks unto our Lord God.

Answer. It is meet and right so to do.

Then shall the Priest turn to the Lord's Table, and say:

IT is very meet, right, and our bounden duty, that we should at all times, and in all places, give thanks unto thee, O Lord, Holy Father, Almighty, Everlasting God.

THEREFORE with Angels and Archangels, and with all the company of heaven, we laud and magnify thy glorious Name; evermore praising thee, and saying, Holy, holy, holy, Lord God of hosts, heaven and earth are full of thy glory: Glory be to thee, O Lord most High. Amen.]

Then shall the Priest, kneeling down at the Lord's Table, say in the name of all them that shall receive the Communion this Prayer following:

WE do not presume to come to this thy Table, O merciful Lord, trusting in our own righteousness, but in thy manifold and great mercies. We are not worthy so much as to gather up the crumbs under thy Table. But thou art the same Lord, whose property is always to have mercy: Grant us therefore, gracious Lord, so to eat the flesh of thy dear Son Jesus Christ, and to drink his blood, that our sinful bodies may be made clean by his body, and our souls washed through his most precious blood, and that we may evermore dwell in him, and he in us. *Amen.*

[When the Priest, standing before the Table, hath so ordered the Bread and Wine, that he may with the more readiness and decency break the Bread before the people, and take the Cup into his hands, he shall saying the Prayer of Consecration, as followeth:

ALMIGHTY God, our heavenly Father, who of thy tender mercy didst give thine only Son Jesus Christ to suffer death upon the Cross for our redemption; who made there (by his one oblation of himself once offered) a full, perfect, and sufficient sacrifice, oblation, and satisfaction, for the sins of the whole world; and did institute, and in his holy Gospel command us to continue, a perpetual memory of that his precious death until his coming again; Hear us, O merciful Father, we most humbly beseech thee; and grant that we receiving these thy creatures of bread and wine, according to thy Son our Saviour Jesus Christ's holy institution, in remembrance of his death and passion, may . be partakers of his most blessed Body and Blood: who, in the same night that he was betrayed, a took Bread; and, when he had given thanks, b he brake it, and gave it to his disciples, saying, Take, eat, c this is my Body which is given for you: Do this in remembrance of me. Likewise after supper he d took the Cup; and, when he had given thanks, he gave it to them saying, Drink ye all of this; for this e is my Blood of the New Testament, which is shed for you and for many for the remission of sins: Do this, as oft as ye shall drink it, in remembrance of me. *Amen.*]

a *Here the Priest is to take the Paten into his hands:*

b *And here to break the Bread:*

c *And here to lay his hand upon all the Bread.*

d *Here he is to take the Cup into his hand:*

e *And here to lay his hand upon every vessel (be it Chalice or Flagon) in which there is any Wine to be consecrated.*

At the time of the distribution of the holy Sacrament, the Priest shall [first receive the Communion himself, and after] minister unto [them that are appointed to communicate with the sick, and last of all to] the sick person. And when he delivereth the Bread [to any one,] he shall say:

THE Body of our Lord Jesus Christ, which was given for thee, preserve thy body and soul unto everlasting life. Take and eat this in remembrance that Christ died for thee, and feed on him in thy heart by faith with thanksgiving.

[And the Minister that delivereth the Cup to any one shall say:

THE Blood of our Lord Jesus Christ, which was shed for thee, preserve thy body and soul unto everlasting life. Drink this in remembrance that Christ's Blood was shed for thee, and be thankful.]

Then shall the Priest say the Lord's Prayer, the people repeating after him every Petition.

OUR Father, which art in heaven, Hallowed be thy Name. Thy kingdom come. Thy will be done, in earth as it is in heaven. Give us this day our daily bread. And forgive us our trespasses, As we forgive them that trespass against us. And lead us not into temptation; But deliver us from evil: For thine is the kingdom, The power, and the glory, For ever and ever. Amen.

[After shall be said as followeth:

O LORD and heavenly Father, we thy humble servants entirely desire thy fatherly goodness mercifully to accept this our sacrifice of praise and thanksgiving; most humbly beseeching thee to grant, that by the merits and death of thy Son Jesus Christ, and through faith in his blood, we and all thy whole Church may obtain remission of our sins, and all other benefits of his passion. And here we offer and present unto thee, O Lord, ourselves, our souls and bodies, to be a reasonable, holy, and lively sacrifice unto thee; humbly beseeching thee, that all we, who are partakers of this holy Communion, may be fulfilled with thy grace and heavenly benediction. And although we be unworthy, through our manifold sins, to offer unto thee any sacrifice, yet we beseech thee to accept this our bounden duty and service; not weighing our merits but pardoning our offences, through Jesus Christ our Lord; by whom, and with whom, in the unity of the Holy Ghost, all honour and glory be unto thee, O Father Almighty, world without end. *Amen.*]

Or this:

A LMIGHTY and everliving God, we most heartily thank thee, for that thou dost vouchsafe to feed us, who have duly received these holy mysteries, with the spiritual food of the most precious Body and Blood of thy Son our Saviour Jesus Christ; and dost assure us thereby of thy favour and goodness towards us; and that we are very members incorporate in the mystical body of thy Son, which is the blessed company of all faithful people; and are also heirs through hope of thy everlasting kingdom, by the merits of the most precious death and passion of thy dear Son. And we most humbly beseech thee, O heavenly Father, so to assist us with thy grace, that we may continue in that holy fellowship, and do all such good works as thou hast prepared for us to walk in; through Jesus Christ our Lord, to whom, with thee and the Holy Ghost, be all honour and glory, world without and. *Amen.*

[*Then shall be said*:

G LORY be to God on high, and in earth peace, good will towards men. We praise thee, we bless thee, we worship thee, we glorify thee, we give thanks to thee for thy great glory, O Lord God, heavenly King, God the Father Almighty.

O Lord, the only-begotten Son Jesus Christ; O Lord God, Lamb of God, Son of the Father, that takest away the sins of the world, have mercy upon us. Thou that takest away the sins of the world, have mercy upon us. Thou that takest away the sins of the world, receive our prayer. Thou that sittest at the right hand of God the Father, have mercy upon us.

For thou only art holy; thou only art the Lord; thou only, O Christ, with the Holy Ghost, art most high in the glory of God the Father. *Amen.*]

Then the Priest shall let them depart with this Blessing.

THE peace of God, which passeth all understanding, keep your hearts and minds in the knowledge and love of God, and of his Son Jesus Christ our Lord: and the blessing of God Almighty, the Father, the Son, and the Holy Ghost, be amongst you and remain with you always. *Amen.*

E

THE ORDER OF ADMINISTERING
THE SACRAMENT OF EXTREME UNCTION

In case of necessity, it suffices to anoint one sense only, or more fittingly the forehead, with this shorter form :

Through this holy Unct ✠ ion the Lord pardon thee whatsoever thou hast done amiss. Amen.

But the obligation remains, when the danger ceases, of supplying each of the anointings and all the prayers. If there be doubt whether the sick person yet lives, the Priest shall anoint conditionally saying :

If thou livest, through this holy Unct ✠ ion, etc.

1. *The Priest, who is to minister the Sacrament of Extreme Unction, shall take care that there be made ready, as far as possible, in the sick man's house, a table covered with a white cloth, and a vessel, wherein is cotton-wool or the like, divided into six small pellets, for wiping the places anointed; bread crumbs for cleansing the fingers; water for washing the Priest's hands, and a wax candle, to give him light as he anoints.*

2. *Then with the Clergy or at least with one Clerk, who carries the Cross without its shaft, the holy Water with sprinkler, and the Ritual, the Parish Priest himself takes the vessel of sacred Oil, enclosed in a bag of violet silk, and carries it with care; for greater safety he may hang it around his neck. No bell is rung.*

3. *When he comes to the place where the sick person lies, the Priest entering the room, says:*

℣. Peace be to this house.

℞. And to all that dwell in it.

4. *Having placed the Oil upon the table, and (if not already vested) having put on surplice and violet stole, the Priest gives the sick man a Cross to kiss. Then he shall sprinkle him, the bystanders, and the room, in the form of a Cross, saying:*

THOU shalt purge me, O Lord, with hyssop, and I shall be clean; thou shalt wash me, and I shall be whiter than snow.

If the sick person wishes to confess, he shall hear him and absolve him. Then he shall comfort him, and if time permit briefly admonish him concerning the power and efficacy of this Sacrament.

5. *Then he says:*

℣. Our help is in the name of the Lord.

℞. Who hath made heaven and earth.

℣. The Lord be with you.

℞. And with thy spirit.

Let us pray.   *Collect.*

LET there enter into this house, O Lord Jesu Christ, with the coming of us unworthy, everlasting happiness, divine prosperity, serene gladness, fruitful charity and everlasting health: let no evil spirits approach this place: may Angels of peace be present and all evil discord far removed from this house: magnify upon us thy holy name, O Lord, and ble ✠ ss our conversation; sanctify our unworthy coming, who art holy and gracious, and abidest with the Father and the Holy Ghost, world without end. ℟. Amen.

LET us pray and beseech our Lord Jesus Christ, that in blessing he may ble ✠ ss this dwelling-place, and all that inhabit it, and give to them a good Angel guardian, and make them so to serve him that they may consider the wondrous things of his law: may he turn from them all adverse powers: deliver them from all fear, and from every disquiet, and vouchsafe to preserve them in safety in this dwelling-place: Who with the Father and the Holy Ghost liveth and reigneth, world without end. ℟. Amen.

Let us pray.   *Collect.*

GRACIOUSLY hear us, O Lord holy, Father almighty, everlasting God: and vouchsafe to send from heaven thy holy Angel to guard and cherish, protect, visit and defend all who dwell in this dwelling-place. Through Christ, our Lord.

℟. Amen.

6. *These prayers, if time does not allow, may be omitted in whole or in part. Then the general Confession is made in the accustomed manner, and the Priest says in the singular number:*

ALMIGHTY God have mercy upon thee (*or if there be several* you), etc. The almighty . . . grant unto thee. (Page 48).

7. *The Priest, extending his right hand over the head of the sick person, says:*

IN the name of the Fa ✠ ther, and of the S ✠ on, and of the Holy ✠ Ghost, may there be extinguished in thee all power of the devil, through the imposition of our hands, and through the invocation of the glorious and holy Virgin Mary Mother of God, and of her illustrious Spouse Joseph, and of all the holy Angels, Archangels, Patriarchs, Prophets, Apostles, Martyrs, Confessors and Virgins, and of all the Saints. Amen.

8. *Then, dipping his thumb in the holy Oil, he anoints the sick person in the form of a Cross on the parts mentioned below, adapting the words of the form to the appropriate place in this manner:*

At the eyes.

Through this holy Unct ✠ ion, and his most tender mercy, the Lord pardon thee whatsoever thou hast done amiss by seeing. Amen.

9. *The Clerk, if he be in Holy Orders, or the Priest himself, after each anointing shall wipe the place anointed with a fresh pellet of cotton-wool, and place it in a clean vessel, and afterwards carry it to the Church, burn it, and cast the ashes into the sacrarium.*

At the ears.

Through this holy Unct ✠ ion, and his most tender mercy, the Lord pardon thee whatsoever thou hast done amiss by hearing. Amen.

At the nostrils.

Through this holy Unct ✠ ion, and his most tender mercy, the Lord pardon thee whatsoever thou hast done amiss by smelling.   Amen.

At the mouth, the lips being closed.

Through this holy Unct ✠ ion, and his most tender mercy, the Lord pardon thee whatsoever thou hast done amiss by tasting and speaking. Amen.

At the hands.

Through this holy Unct ✠ ion, and his most tender mercy, the Lord pardon thee whatsoever thou hast done amiss by touching.   Amen.

10.   *And note, that the hands of Priests are not anointed on the inside, but on the outside.*

At the feet.

Through this holy Unct ✠ ion, and his most tender mercy, the Lord pardon thee whatsoever thou hast done amiss by walking.   Amen.

11.   *This Unction of the feet may be omitted for any reasonable cause.*

12.   *All these things being done, the Priest rubs his thumb with bread crumbs, washes his hands, and wipes them with the towel. The water and bread shall in due course be cast into the sacrarium or the fire.   Then he says:*

Kyrie, eléison.
Christe, eléison.
Kyrie, eléison.

Our Father. *(secretly)*.

℣. And lead us not into temptation.
℟. But deliver us from evil.
℣. O Lord, save thy servant (handmaid).
℟. Who putteth *his* trust in thee.
℣. Send *him* help from thy holy place.
℟. And evermore mightily defend *him*.
℣. Be unto *him,* O Lord, a tower of strength.
℟. From the face of the enemy.
℣. Let the enemy have no advantage over *him*.
℟. Nor the wicked approach to hurt *him*.
℣. O Lord, hear my prayer.
℟. And let my cry come unto thee.
℣. The Lord be with you.
℟. And with thy spirit.

Let us pray.   *Collect.*

O LORD God, who through thine Apostle James hast said : Is any sick among you? Let him call for the elders of the Church, and let them pray over him, anointing him with oil in the name of the Lord : and the prayer of faith shall save the sick, and the Lord shall raise him up : and if he have committed sins, they shall be forgiven him ; cure, we beseech thee, O our Redeemer, by the grace of the Holy Ghost, the weakness of this sick person, heal *his* wounds and put away *his* sins ; cast out from *him* all pains of mind and body, and mercifully give back to *him* full health, both inwardly and outwardly, that, being restored by the help of thy mercy, *he* may return to *his* duties as of old : Who with the Father and the same Holy Ghost livest and reignest God, world without end. ℟. **Amen.**

Let us pray.   *Collect.*

LOOK, O Lord, we beseech thee, upon this thy servant N. . . . (handmaid N.) languishing in weakness of body, and comfort again the soul which thou hast created : that, being amended by thy chastisement, *he* may feel *himself* to be saved by thy healing. Through Christ, our Lord. ℟. Amen.

Let us pray.   *Collect.*

O LORD holy, Father almighty, everlasting God, who in pouring the grace of thy blessing upon sick bodies dost preserve by thy manifold goodness thy handy-work : graciously assist us who call upon thy name ; deliver thy servant (handmaid) from *his* sickness, and give *him* health ; raise *him* up by thy right hand ; strengthen *him* by thy might ; protect *him* by thy power ; and with all the prosperity which *he* desires restore *him* to thy holy Church. Through Christ, our Lord. ℟. Amen.

During the anointings the bystanders should say suitable prayers for the sick man, e.g., one or more of the Penitential Psalms (6, 32, 38, 51, 102, 130, 143) or the Litanies of the Saints (page 74).

13. *At the end he may give brief and salutary exhortations to enable the sick person to die in the Lord and to strengthen him to put to flight the temptations of evil spirits.*

14. *Finally he should leave with him holy Water and a Cross that he may frequently look upon it, and according to his devotion kiss it and embrace it.*

15. *He should also warn the relatives and servants of the sick man to send at once for the Parish Priest, if the disease grows worse, that he may help the dying man, and commend his soul to God; but if death is at hand, the Priest, before he departs, shall duly commend the soul to God.*

16. *When this Sacrament is administered to several sick persons at the same time, the Priest shall present the Cross to each to be devoutly kissed, and shall say all the prayers which precede and follow the anointing once for all in the plural number; but he shall perform the anointings with their respective forms separately on each sick person.*

LITANIES OF THE SAINTS

When the Litanies are sung in Procession, each Petition is sung in full twice, first by the Cantors and then by the Clergy : but otherwise it is sung or said once only.

Before the Procession (the Celebrant standing at the Altar steps) is recited :

ANT : O Lord, arise, help us and deliver us for thy name's sake. *Ps.* O God, we have heard with our ears : * our fathers have declared unto us.

Glory be. *And repeat,* O Lord, arise.

Then all kneel: the Procession begins at the singing of Holy Mary.

KYRIE, eléison.
Christe, eléison.
Kyrie, eléison.
O Christ, hear us.
O Christ, graciously hear us.
O God the Father of heaven, have mercy upon us.
O God the Son, Redeemer of the world, have mercy upon us.
O God the Holy Ghost, have mercy upon us.
Holy Trinity, one God, have mercy upon us.

Holy Mary.
           pray for us.
Holy Mother of God,   pray.
Holy Virgin of virgins,   pray.
St. Michael,   pray.
St. Gabriel,   pray.
St. Raphael,   pray.
All ye holy Angels and Archangels,
           pray for us.
All ye holy orders of blessed Spirits,   pray.
St. John the Baptist,
St. Joseph,   pray.

All ye holy Patriarchs
and Prophets,
pray for us.

St. Peter, pray.
St. Paul, pray.
St. Andrew, pray.
*St. James, pray.
St. John, pray.
*St. Thomas, pray.
*St. James, pray.
*S. Philip, pray.
*St. Bartholomew, pray.
*St. Matthew, pray.
*St. Simon, pray.
*St. Jude, pray.
*St. Matthias, pray.
*St. Barnabas, pray.
*St. Luke, pray.
*St. Mark, pray.

All ye holy Apostles
and Evangelists,
pray for us.

All ye holy Disciples
of the Lord, pray.
*All ye holy
Innocents, pray.
St. Stephen, pray.
St. Laurence, pray.
St. Vincent, pray.
*St. Fabian and
St. Sebastian, pray.

*St. John and
St. Paul, pray.
*St. Cosmas and
St. Damian, pray.
*St. Gervase and
St. Protase, pray.

All ye holy
Martyrs, pray.
St. Silvester, pray.
St. Gregory, pray.
*St. Ambrose, pray.
St. Augustine, pray.
*St. Jerome, pray.
*St. Martin, pray.
*St. Nicholas, pray.

All ye holy Bishops
and Confessors, pray.

All ye holy
Doctors, pray.
St. Anthony, pray.
St. Benedict, pray.
*St. Bernard, pray.
St. Dominic, pray.
St. Francis, pray.

All ye holy Priests
and Levites,

All ye holy Monks
and Hermits, pray.
St. Mary Magdalen, pray.
†St. Agatha, pray.

* = omitted on Vigils of Easter and Pentecost.

*St. Lucy,   pray.
 St. Agnes,   pray.
 St. Cæcilia,   pray.
*St. Catherine,   pray.
 St. Anastasia,   pray.
 All ye holy Virgins
   and Widows,   pray.
 All ye holy men and
   women, Saints of
   God, intercede for us.
 Be merciful, spare us,
                            O Lord.
 Be merciful, graciously
                hear us, O Lord.
 From all evil,
         deliver us, O Lord.
 From all sin,   deliver.
*From thy wrath,
                      deliver.
*From sudden and
   unprepared death,
                      deliver.
*From the crafts of
   the devil,   deliver.
*From anger, hatred,
   and all uncharitable-
   ness,   deliver.
*From the spirit of
   uncleanness,   deliver.

*From lightning and
   tempest,   deliver.
*From the scourge of
   earthquake,   deliver.
*From pestilence, famine,
   and war,   deliver.
 From everlasting
   death,   deliver.
 Through the mystery of
   thy holy Incarnation,
                      deliver.
 Through thine
   advent,   deliver.
 Through thy
   nativity,   deliver.
 Through thy baptism
   and holy fasting,
                      deliver.
 Through thy cross
   and passion,   deliver.
 Through thy death
   and burial,   deliver.
 Through thy holy
   resurrection,   deliver.
 Through thy wonder-
   ful ascension,   deliver.
 Through the coming
   of the Holy Ghost
   the Paraclete,   deliver.

* = omitted on Vigils of Easter and Pentecost.
† In the shorter Litanies the order is: St. Agnes, St. Cæcilia,
St. Agatha.

In the day of judgment, deliver us, O Lord.

We sinners, ℟. beseech thee to hear us.

That thou wouldest spare us, ℟. we beseech thee, hear us.

*That thou wouldest pardon us, we beseech.

*That it may please thee to bring us to true repentance, we beseech.

That it may please thee to govern and preserve thy holy Church,
we beseech.

That it may please thee to preserve our Apostolic lord and all orders of the Church in holy religion, we beseech thee, hear us.

That it may please thee to humble the enemies of holy Church,
we beseech.

That it may please thee to give unto Christian kings and rulers peace and true concord,
we beseech.

*That it may please thee to grant to all Christian people peace and unity, we beseech thee, hear us.

*That it may please thee to recall such as do err into the unity of the Church, and to bring all unbelievers into the light of the gospel, we beseech thee, hear us.

That it may please thee to strengthen, and preserve us in thy holy service, we beseech thee, hear us.

*That thou wouldest lift up our minds unto heavenly desires,
we beseech.

That thou wouldest reward all our benefactors with everlasting blessings, we beseech thee, hear us.

*That thou wouldest deliver our souls, and the souls of our brethren, kinsfolk, and

* = omitted on Vigils of Easter and Pentecost.

benefactors, f r o m eternal damnation,
> we beseech.

That it may please thee to give and preserve the fruits of the earth, we beseech thee, hear us.

That it may please thee to grant unto all the faithful departed rest eternal, we beseech thee, hear us.

That it may please thee graciously to hear us, we beseech thee, hear us.

Son of God, we beseech thee, hear us.

O Lamb of God, who takest away the sins of the world, spare us, O Lord.

O Lamb of God, who takest away the sins of the world, graciously hear us, O Lord.

O Lamb of God, who takest away the sins of the world, have mercy upon us.

O Christ hear us.

*O Christ, graciously hear us.

Kyrie, eléison.

Christe, eléison.

Kyrie, eléison.

Our Father, *secretly as far as*

℣. And lead us not into temptation.

℟. But deliver us from evil.

Ps. 70. *Deus in adjustorium.*

HASTE thee, O God, to deliver me: * make haste to help me, O Lord.

Let them be ashamed and confounded that seek after my soul: * let them be turned backward and put to confusion that wish me evil.

* = On the Vigils of Easter and Pentecost the Litanies end here.

Let them for their reward be soon brought to shame: * that cry over me, There, there.

But let all those that seek thee be joyful and glad in thee: * and let all such as delight in thy salvation say alway, The Lord be praised.

As for me, I am poor and in misery: * haste thee unto me, O God.

Thou art my helper and my redeemer: * O Lord, make no long tarrying.

Glory be.　　　As it was.

℣. Save thy servants.

℞. My God, who put their trust in thee.

℣. Be unto us, O Lord, a strong tower.

℞. From the face of the enemy.

℣. Let the enemy have no advantage over us.

℞. Nor the son of wickedness approach to hurt us.

℣. O Lord, deal not with us after our sins.

℞. Neither reward us after our iniquities.

℣. Let us pray for our Chief Bishop, N.

℞. The Lord preserve him and keep him alive, and make him blessed upon earth, and deliver him not up to the will of his enemies.

℣. Let us pray for our benefactors.

℞. Vouchsafe, O Lord, for thy name's sake, to reward with eternal life all those who do us good. Amen.

℣. Let us pray for the faithful departed.

℞. Rest eternal grant unto them, O Lord, and let light perpetual shine upon them.

℣.   May they rest in peace.

℟.   Amen.

℣.   For our absent brethren.

℟.   My God, save thy servants who put their trust in thee.

℣.   O Lord, send them help from thy holy place.

℟.   And from Sion protect them.

℣.   O Lord, hear my prayer.

℟.   And let my cry come unto thee.

(The Priest alone stands.)

℣.   The Lord be with you.

℟.   And with thy spirit.

Let us pray.   *Collect.*

O GOD to whom only it belongs ever to have mercy and to forgive: receive our humble petitions; that we and all thy servants who are bound by the chains of sin, through thy merciful loving-kindness may graciously be absolved.

WE beseech thee, O Lord, mercifully to hear the prayers of thy humble servants, and to forgive them the sins of them that confess the same unto thee: that they may obtain of thy loving-kindness, pardon and peace.

GRACIOUSLY shew forth upon us, O Lord, thy unspeakable mercy : that thou wouldest both loose us from all our sins, and likewise deliver us from the punishment which for the same we deserve.

O GOD, who art wroth with them that sin against thee, and sparest them that are penitent: mercifully look upon the prayers of thy people who call upon thee; and turn away the scourges of thy wrath, which for our sins we justly deserve.

ALMIGHTY and everlasting God, have mercy upon thy servant N., our Chief Bishop, and, according to thy great goodness, direct him into the way of everlasting salvation: that, by thy grace, he may desire that which is well pleasing unto thee, and with all his strength perform the same.

O GOD, from whom all holy desires, all right counsels, and all just actions proceed: grant that peace to thy servants which the world cannot give, that both, our hearts may be set to obey thy commandments, and also that we, being defended from the fear of our enemies, may pass our time in quietness under thy protection.

KINDLE, O Lord, with the fire of the Holy Spirit our reins and our hearts : that we may serve thee with a chaste body, and please thee with a clean heart.

O GOD, the Creator and Redeemer of all the faithful, grant unto the souls of thy servants and handmaidens the remission of all their sins: that through devout supplications they may obtain the pardon which they have always desired.

F

PREVENT us, O Lord, we beseech thee, in our doings with thy most gracious favour, and further us with thy continual help : that all our prayer and work may be begun, continued and ended in thee.

ALMIGHTY and everlasting God, who hast dominion both of the living and of the dead, and hast mercy upon all whom thou foreknowest will be thine in faith and works: we humbly beseech thee; that all those for whom we are minded to pour forth our prayers, whether in this present world they still be held in the flesh, or being delivered from the body have passed into that which is to come, may at the intercession of all the Saints obtain of thy bountiful goodness the remission of all their sins.   Through.

℣.   The Lord be with you.

℟.   And with thy spirit.

℣.   (*Cantors.*)   May the almighty and merciful Lord graciously hear us.

℟.   Amen.

℣.   And may the souls of the faithful through the mercy of God rest in peace.

℟.   Amen.

IN TIME OF WAR.

The Litanies of the Saints as above, as far as

℣. And lead us not into temptation.

℟. But deliver us from evil.

PSALM 46. *Deus noster refugium.*

GOD is our hope and strength : * a very present help in trouble.

Therefore will we not fear, though the earth be moved : * and though the hills be carried into the midst of the sea.

Though the waters thereof rage and swell: * and though the mountains shake at the tempest of the same.

The rivers of the flood thereof shall make glad the city of God: * the holy place of the tabernacle of the most Highest.

God is in the midst of her, therefore shall she not be removed: * God shall help her, and that right early.

The heathen make much ado, and the kingdoms are moved: * but God hath shewed his voice, and the earth shall melt away.

The Lord of hosts is with us: * the God of Jacob is our refuge.

O come hither, and behold the works of the Lord: * what destruction he hath brought upon the earth.

He maketh wars to cease in all the world: he breaketh the bow, and snappeth the spear in sunder: * and burneth the chariots in the fire.

Be still then and know that I am God: * I will be exalted among the heathen, and I will be exalted in the earth.

The Lord of hosts is with us: * the God of Jacob is our refuge.

Glory be. As it was.

℣. Arise, O Lord, and help us.

℟. And deliver us for thy name's sake.

℣. Save thy people, O Lord.

℟. Who put their trust in thee, O my God.

℣. In thy strength let there be peace.

℟. And plenty in thy towers.

℣. Be unto us, O Lord, a strong tower.

℟. From the face of the enemy.

℣. He shall break the bow and snap the weapons in sunder.

℟. And the shields shall he burn in the fire.

℣. O Lord, send us help from thy holy place.

℟. And from Sion protect us.

℣. O Lord, hear my prayer.

℟. And let my cry come unto thee.

Let us pray.   *Collect.*

O GOD, who makest wars to cease, and, by thy powerful defence, dost defeat the foes of them that put their trust in thee : assist thy servants who implore thy mercy ; that the fierceness of their enemies being overthrown, we may praise thee with continual thanksgiving.

O GOD, from whom all holy desires, all right counsels, and all just actions proceed : grant that peace to thy servants which the world cannot give ; that both, our hearts may be set to obey thy commandments, and also that we, being defended from the fear of our enemies, may pass our time in quietness under thy protection.

WE beseech thee, O Lord, to bring down the pride of our enemies : and by the right hand of thy power overthrow their obstinacy. Through. ℞. Amen.

VISITATION OF THE SICK

All the following prayers may be said or omitted at the discretion of the Priest, as time and the condition of the sick person may demand.

1. *Upon entering the sick person's room the Priest says:*

℣. Peace be to this house.

℟. And to all that dwell in it.

2. *In the sick room the Priest sprinkles the sick person, the bed and the room, and says:—*

THOU shalt purge me, O Lord, with hyssop, and I shall be clean : thou shalt wash me and I shall be whiter than snow.

Then he ministers to the sick person in this or other like manner. And he may say the following Psalm over the sick person:

PSALM 91. *Qui habitat.*

WHOSO dwelleth under the defence of the most High : * shall abide under the shadow of the Almighty.

I will say unto the Lord, Thou art my hope, and my strong hold : * my God, in him will I trust.

For he shall deliver thee from the snare of the hunter : * and from the noisome pestilence.

He shall defend thee under his wings, and thou shalt be safe under his feathers: * his faithfulness and truth shall be thy shield and buckler.

Thou shalt not be afraid for any terror by night : * nor for the arrow that flieth by day.

For the pestilence that walketh in darkness : * nor for the sickness that destroyeth in the noonday.

A thousand shall fall beside thee, and ten thousand at thy right hand : * but it shall not come nigh thee.

Yea, with thine eyes shalt thou behold : * and see the reward of the ungodly.

For thou, Lord, art my hope : * thou hast set thine house of defence very high.

There shall no evil happen unto thee : * neither shall any plague come nigh thy dwelling.

For he shall give his Angels charge over thee: * to keep thee in all thy ways.

They shall bear thee in their hands : * that thou hurt not thy foot against a stone.

Thou shalt go upon the lion and adder : * the young lion and the dragon shalt thou tread under thy feet.

Because he hath set his love upon me, therefore will I deliver him : * I will set him up, because he hath known my Name.

He shall call upon me, and I will hear him : * yea, I am with him in trouble ; I will deliver him, and bring him to honour.

With long life will I satisfy him : * and shew him my salvation.

Glory be. As it was.

Kyrie, eléison. Christe, eléison. Kyrie, eléison.

Our Father *(secretly)*.

℣.   And lead us not into temptation.
℟.   But deliver us from evil.

℣.   Save thy servant (handmaid).
℟.   My God, who trusteth in thee.

℣.   Send *him* help, O Lord, from the holy
      place.
℟.   And strengthen *him* out of Sion.

℣.   Let the enemy have no advantage over
      him.
℟.   Nor the son of wickedness have power to
      hurt *him*.

℣.   Be unto *him*, O Lord, a tower of strength.
℟.   From the face of the enemy.

℣.   The Lord comfort *him*.
℟.   When he lieth sick upon *his* bed.

℣.   O Lord, hear my prayer.
℟.   And let my cry come unto thee.

℣.   The Lord be with you.
℟.   And with thy spirit.

Let us pray.   *Collect.*

O GOD, whose property is ever to have mercy
and to forgive: receive our supplication; that
we and this thy servant (this thy handmaid), who
are tied and bound by the chains of our sins, may
by the pitifulness of thy great mercy be loosed
from the same.

O GOD, the only support of the frailty of men,
shew forth the might of thy succour on this thy

servant (this thy handmaid) who is sick : that by the help of thine availing mercy *he* may be worthy to be restored in health to thy holy Church.

GRANT, we beseech thee, O Lord God, that this thy servant (this thy handmaid) may enjoy perpetual health of mind and body : and, at the glorious intercession of blessed Mary ever Virgin, be delivered from present sadness, and rejoice in everlasting gladness. Through Christ, our Lord. Ṛ. Amen.

The blessing of God almighty, the Father, the Son, ✠ and the Holy Ghost, descend upon thee, and abide with thee alway. Ṛ. Amen.

Then he sprinkles him (her) with holy Water.

---

3. *Any of the following Psalms and Gospels may be read at the discretion of the Priest or the desire of the sick person; and before any Gospel the Priest shall say :*

Ỿ. The Lord be with you.

Ṛ. And with thy spirit.

And signing himself and, if he be a male, likewise the sick person, if he cannot sign himself.

Ỿ. The Continuation of the holy Gospel according to N.

Ṛ. Glory be to thee, O Lord.

Psalm 6. Matt. 8, 5-13.
Psalm 16. Mark 16, 14-18.
Psalm 20. Luke 4, 38-40.
Psalm 86. John 5, 1-14.
Psalm 91. John 1, 1-14.

THE ORDER FOR
VISITATION OF THE SICK

(ACCORDING TO THE BOOK OF COMMON PRAYER.)

When any person is sick, notice shall be given thereof to the Minister of the Parish, who, coming into the sick person's house, shall say:

PEACE be to this house, and to all that dwell in it.

When he cometh into the sick man's presence he shall say, kneeling down:

REMEMBER not, Lord, our iniquities, nor the iniquities of our forefathers: Spare us, good Lord, spare thy people, whom thou hast redeemed with thy most precious blood, and be not angry with us for ever.

Answer. Spare us, good Lord,

Then the Minister shall say:

Let us pray.

Lord have mercy upon us.

Christ have mercy upon us.

Lord have mercy upon us.

OUR Father, which art in heaven, Hallowed be thy Name. Thy kingdom come. Thy will be done, in earth as it is in heaven. Give us this day our daily bread. And forgive us our trespasses, As we forgive them that trespass against us. And lead us not into temptation but deliver us from evil. Amen.

Minister. O Lord, save thy servant.
Answer. Which putteth *his* trust in thee.

Minister. Send *him* help from thy holy place;
Answer. And evermore mightily defend *him*.

Minister. Let the enemy have no advantage of *him;*
Answer. Nor the wicked approach to hurt *him*.

Minister. Be unto *him*, O Lord, a strong tower.
Answer. From the face of *his* enemy.

Minister. O Lord, hear our prayers.
Answer. And let our cry come unto thee.

Minister.

O LORD, look down from heaven, behold, visit, and relieve this thy servant. Look upon *him* with the eyes of thy mercy, give *him* comfort and sure confidence in thee, defend *him* from the danger of the enemy, and keep *him* in perpetual peace and safety; through Jesus Christ our Lord. *Amen.*

HEAR us, Almighty and most merciful God and Saviour; extend thy accustomed goodness to this thy servant who is grieved with sickness. Sanctify, we beseech thee, this thy fatherly correction to *him;* that the sense of *his* weakness may add strength to *his* faith, and seriousness to *his* repentance: That, if it shall be thy good pleasure to restore *him* to *his* former health, *he* may lead the residue of *his* life in *thy* fear, and to thy glory: or else, give *him* grace so to take thy visitation, that, after this painful life ended, *he* may dwell with thee in life everlasting; through Jesus Christ our Lord. *Amen.*

Then shall the Minister exhort the sick person after this form, or other like.

DEARLY beloved, know this, that Almighty God is the Lord of life and death, and of all things to them pertaining, as youth, strength, health, age, weakness, and sickness. Wherefore, whatsoever your sickness is, know you certainly, that it is God's visitation. And for what cause soever this sickness is sent unto you; whether it be to try your patience for the example of others, and that your faith may be found in the day of the Lord laudable, glorious, and honourable, to the increase of glory and endless felicity; or else it be sent unto you to correct and amend in you whatsoever doth offend the eyes of your heavenly Father; know you certainly, that if you truly repent you of your sins, and bear your sickness patiently, trusting in God's mercy, for his dear Son Jesus Christ's sake, and render unto him humble thanks for his fatherly visitation, submitting yourself wholly unto his will, it shall turn to your profit, and help you forward in the right way that leadeth unto everlasting life.

If the person visited be very sick, then the Curate may end his exhortation in this place, or else proceed.

TAKE therefore in good part the chastisement of the Lord: For (as Saint Paul saith in the twelfth Chapter to the Hebrews) whom the Lord loveth he chasteneth, and scourgeth every son whom he receiveth. If ye endure chastening, God dealeth with you as with sons; for what son is he whom the father chasteneth not? But if ye be without chastisement, whereof all are partakers, then are ye bastards, and not sons. Furthermore, we have had fathers of our flesh, which corrected us, and we gave them reverence: shall we not much rather be in subjection unto the Father of spirits, and live? For they verily for a few days chastened us after their

own pleasure; but he for our profit, that we might
be partakers of his holiness. These words, good
brother, are written in holy Scripture for our comfort
and instruction; that we should patiently, and with
thanksgiving, bear our heavenly Father's correction,
whensoever by any manner of adversity it shall
please his gracious goodness to visit us. And there
should be no greater comfort to Christian persons,
than to be made like unto Christ, by suffering
patiently adversities, troubles, and sicknesses. For
he himself went not up to joy, but first he suffered
pain; he entered not into his glory before he was
crucified. So truly our way to eternal joy is to suffer
here with Christ; and our door to enter into eternal
life is gladly to die with Christ; that we may rise
again from death, and dwell with him in everlasting
life. Now, therefore, taking your sickness, which is
thus profitable for you, patiently, I exhort you, in the
Name of God, to remember the profession which you
made unto God in your Baptism. And forasmuch as
after this life there is an account to be given unto
the righteous Judge, by whom all must be judged,
without respect of persons, I require you to examine
yourself and your estate, both toward God and man;
so that, accusing and condemning yourself for your
own faults, you may find mercy at our heavenly
Father's hand for Christ's sake, and not be accused
and condemned in that fearful judgment. Therefore
I shall rehearse to you the Articles of our Faith, that
you may know whether you do believe as a Christian
man should, or no.

*Here the Minister shall rehearse the Articles of the
Faith, saying thus:*

DOST thou believe in God the Father Almighty,
Maker of heaven and earth? And in Jesus

Christ his only-begotten Son our Lord? And that he was conceived by the Holy Ghost, born of the Virgin Mary; that he suffered under Pontius Pilate, was crucified, dead, and buried; that he went down into hell, and also did rise again the third day; that he ascended into heaven, and sitteth at the right hand of God the Father Almighty; and from thence shall come again at the end of the world, to judge the quick and the dead?

And dost thou believe in the Holy Ghost; the holy Catholick Church; the Communion of Saints; the Remission of sins; the Resurrection of the flesh; and everlasting life after death?

The sick person shall answer:

All this I stedfastly believe.

Then shall the Minister examine whether he repent him truly of his sins, and be in charity with all the world; exhorting him to forgive, from the bottom of his heart, all persons that have offended him; and if he hath offended any other, to ask them forgiveness; and where he hath done injury or wrong to any man, that he makes amends to the uttermost of his power. And if he hath not before disposed of his goods, let him then be admonished to make his Will, and to declare his Debts, what he oweth, and what is owing unto him; for the better discharging of his conscience, and the quietness of his Executors. But men should often be put in remembrance to take order for the settling of their temporal estates, whilst they are in health.

These words before rehearsed may be said before the Minister begin his Prayer, as he shall see cause.

The Minister should not omit earnestly to move such sick persons as are of ability to be liberal to the poor.

Here shall the sick person be moved to make a special Confession of his sins, if he feel his conscience troubled with any weighty matter. After which Confession the Priest shall absolve him (if he humbly and heartily desire it) after this sort.

OUR Lord Jesus Christ, who hath left power to his Church to absolve all sinners who truly repent and believe in him, of his great mercy forgive thee thine offences: And by his authority committed to me, I absolve thee from all thy sins, In the Name of the Father, and of the Son, and of the Holy Ghost. Amen.

And then the Priest shall say the Collect following.

Let us pray.

O MOST merciful God, who, according to the multitude of thy mercies, dost so put away the sins of those who truly repent, that thou rememberest them no more; Open thine eye of mercy upon this thy servant, who most earnestly desireth pardon and forgiveness. Renew in *him*, most loving Father, whatsover hath been decayed by the fraud and malice of the devil; or by *his* own carnal will and frailness; preserve and continue this sick member in the unity of the Church; consider *his* contrition, accept *his* tears, asswage *his* pain, as shall seem to thee most expedient for *him*. And forasmuch as *he* putteth *his* full trust only in thy mercy, impute not unto *him his* former sins, but strengthen *him* with thy blessed Spirit; and, when thou art pleased to take *him* hence, take *him* unto thy favour, through the merits of thy most dearly beloved Son Jesus Christ our Lord. *Amen.*

Then shall the Minister say this Psalm.

PSALM 71. *In te, Domine, speravi.*

IN thee, O Lord, have I put my trust; let me never be put to confusion; but rid me, and deliver me in thy righteousness; incline thine ear unto me, and save me.

Be thou my strong hold, whereunto I may alway resort: thou hast promised to help me; for thou art my house of defence, and my castle.

Deliver me, O my God, out of the hand of the ungodly: out of the hand of the unrighteous and cruel man.

For thou, O Lord God, art the thing that I long for: thou art my hope, even from my youth.

Through thee have I been holden up ever since I was born: thou art he that took me out of my mother's womb; my praise shall alway be of thee.

I am become as it were a monster unto many: but my sure trust is in thee.

O let my mouth be filled with thy praise: that I may sing of thy glory and honour all the day long.

Cast me not away in the time of age: forsake me not when my strength faileth me.

For mine enemies speak against me, and they that lay wait for my soul take their counsel together, saying: God hath forsaken him, persecute him, and take him; for there is none to deliver him.

Go not far from me, O God: my God, haste thee to help me.

Let them be confounded and perish that are against my soul: let them be covered with shame and dishonour that seek to do me evil.

As for me, I will patiently abide alway: and will praise thee more and more.

My mouth shall daily speak of thy righteousness and salvation: for I know no end thereof.

I will go forth in the strength of the Lord God: and will make mention of thy righteousness only.

Thou, O God, hast taught me from my youth up until now: therefore will I tell of thy wondrous works.

Forsake me not, O God, in mine old age, when I am gray-headed: until I have shewed thy strength unto this generation, and thy power to all them that are yet for to come.

Thy righteousness, O God, is very high, and great things are they that thou hast done: O God, who is like unto thee?

Glory be to the Father, and to the Son: and to the Holy Ghost;

As it was in the beginning, is now, and ever shall be: world without end. Amen.

Adding this.

O SAVIOUR of the world, who by thy Cross and precious Blood hast redeemed us, Save us, and help us, we humbly beseech thee, O Lord.

Then shall the Minister say:

THE ALMIGHTY Lord, who is a most strong tower to them that put their trust in him, to whom all things in heaven, in earth, and under the earth, do bow and obey, be now and evermore thy defence; and make thee know and feel, that there is none other Name under heaven given to man, in whom, and through whom, thou mayest receive health and salvation, but only the Name of our Lord Jesus Christ. Amen.

And after that shall say:

UNTO God's gracious mercy and protection we commit thee. The Lord bless thee, and keep thee. The Lord make his face to shine upon thee, and be gracious unto thee. The Lord lift up his countenance upon thee, and give thee peace, both now and evermore. *Amen.*

A Prayer for a sick Child.

O ALMIGHTY God, and merciful Father, to whom alone belong the issues of life and death; Look down from heaven, we humbly beseech thee, with the eyes of mercy upon this child now lying upon the bed of sickness: Visit *him*, O Lord, with thy salvation; deliver *him* in thy good appointed time from *his* bodily pain, and save *his* soul for thy mercies' sake: That, if it shall be thy pleasure to prolong *his* days here on earth, *he* may live to thee, and be an instrument of thy glory, by serving thee faithfully, and doing good in *his* generation; or else receive *him* into those heavenly habitations, where the souls of them that sleep in the Lord Jesus enjoy perpetual rest and felicity. Grant this, O Lord, for thy mercies' sake, in the same thy Son our Lord Jesus Christ, who liveth and reigneth with thee and the Holy Ghost, ever one God, world without end. *Amen.*

A Prayer for a sick person, when there appeareth small hope of recovery.

O FATHER of mercies, and God of all comfort, our only help in time of need; We fly unto thee for succour in behalf of this thy servant, here lying under thy hand in great weakness of body. Look graciously upon *him*, O Lord; and the more the outward man decayeth, strengthen *him*, we beseech thee, so much the more continually with thy grace and Holy Spirit in the inner man. Give *him* unfeigned repentance for all the errors of *his* life past, and stedfast faith in thy Son Jesus; that *his* sins may be done away by thy mercy, and *his* pardon sealed in heaven, before *he* go hence, and be no more seen. We know, O Lord, that there is no word impossible with thee; and that, if thou wilt, thou canst even yet raise *him* up, and grant *him* a longer continuance amongst us: Yet, forasmuch as in all appearance the time of *his* dissolution draweth near, so fit and prepare *him*, we beseech thee, against the hour of death, that after *his* departure hence in peace, and in thy favour, *his* soul may be received into thine everlasting kingdom, through the merits and mediation of Jesus Christ, thine only Son, our Lord and Saviour. *Amen.*

A commendatory Prayer for a sick person at the point of departure.

O ALMIGHTY God, with whom do live the spirits of just men made perfect, after they are delivered from their earthly prisons; We humbly commend the soul of this thy servant, our dear *brother*, into thy hands, as into the hands of a faithful Creator, and most merciful Saviour; most humbly beseeching thee, that it may be precious in thy sight. Wash it, we pray thee, in the blood of that immaculate Lamb, that was slain to take away the sins of the world; that whatever defilements it may have contracted in the midst of this miserable and naughty world, through the lusts of the flesh, or the wiles of Satan, being purged and done away, it may be presented pure and without spot before thee. And teach us who survive, in this and other like daily spectacles of mortality, to see how frail and uncertain our own condition is; and so to number our days, that we may seriously apply our hearts to that holy and heavenly wisdom, whilst we live here, which may in the end bring us to life everlasting, through the merits of Jesus Christ thine only Son our Lord. *Amen.*

A Prayer for persons troubled in mind or in conscience.

O BLESSED Lord, the Father of mercies, and the God of all comforts; We beseech thee, look down in pity and compassion upon this thy afflicted servant. Thou writest bitter things against *him*, and makest *him* to possess *his* former iniquities; thy wrath lieth hard upon *him*, and *his* soul is full of trouble: But, O merciful God, who hast written thy holy Word for our learning, that we, through patience and comfort of thy holy Scriptures, might have hope; give *him* a right understanding of *himself*, and of thy threats and promises; that *he* may neither cast away *his* confidence in thee, nor place it any where but in thee. Give *him* strength against all *his* temptations, and heal all *his* distempers. Break not the bruised reed. nor quench the smoking flax. Shut not up thy tender mercies in displeasure; but make *him* to hear of joy and gladness, that the bones which thou hast broken may rejoice. Deliver *him* from fear of the enemy, and lift up the light of thy countenance upon *him*, and give *him* peace, through the merits and mediation of Jesus Christ our Lord. *Amen.*

THE BLESSING OF A SICK CHILD

This office may be suitably used for Infants who, being under seven years of age, may not receive the Sacrament of Extreme Unction.

The Priest, when he comes to the place where the Child is, shall say:

Peace be to this house.

℞. And to all that dwell in it.

Then, in silence he sprinkles the Child, the bystanders, and the room, with holy Water, and this done, recites Psalm 113 (page 153).

Then he says:

> Kyrie, eléison.
> Christe, eléison.
> Kyrie, eléison.

Our Father *(secretly).*

℣. And lead us not into temptation.
℞. But deliver us from evil.

℣. Our God is merciful.
℞. The Lord who preserveth the children.

℣. Suffer little children to come unto me.
℞. For of such is the kingdom of heaven.

℣. O Lord hear my prayer.
℞. And let my cry come unto thee.

℣. The Lord be with you.
℞. And with thy spirit.

Let us pray. *Collect.*

O GOD in whom all things grow, and by whom all that which is come to full stature is made strong: stretch forth thy right hand upon this thy servant (handmaid) who, at this tender age, is stricken with sickness; and grant that, being restored to health and strength, *he* may attain to fulness of years and may serve thee faithfully and thankfully all the days of *his* life. Through. ℞. Amen.

Let us pray. *Collect.*

O FATHER of mercies, and God of all comfort, who dost care for thy creation with manifold loving-kindness, and dost pour forth the grace of healing not only on the soul but also on the body; vouchsafe to raise up this sick child from *his* bed of suffering, and restore *him* whole in mind and body to thy holy Church and to *his* parents; that, growing in wisdom and in favour with thee and with men, *he* may serve thee, all the days that thou shalt add unto *his* life, in holiness and righteousness, and may pay *his* debt of gratitude unto thy mercy. Through Christ, our Lord. ℞. Amen.

Let us pray. *Collect.*

O EVERLASTING God, who hast ordained and constituted the services of Angels and men in a wonderful order; mercifully grant, that as thy holy Angels always do thee service in heaven, so by thy appointment they may succour and defend

the life of this boy (girl) on earth. Through
Christ, our Lord. ℟. Amen.

*And laying his right hand upon the head of the
sick Child, he adds:*

THEY shall lay their hands upon the sick and
they shall recover.

MAY Jesus the Son of Mary, the salvation and
Lord of the world, by the merits and intercession
of his holy Apostles Peter and Paul and all the
Saints, be unto thee merciful and gracious. Amen.

*Then, if time allow, may be read the following
Gospel:*

℣. The Lord be with you.
℟. And with thy spirit.
℣. The Beginning of the holy Gospel
according to John.
℟. Glory be to thee, O Lord.

While the Priest says The Beginning. etc., *he
makes the sign of the Cross as usual upon himself on
forehead, mouth and breast; likewise on the sick
Child, if he cannot sign himself.*

IN the beginning was the Word, and the Word
was with God, and the Word was God. The
same was in the beginning with God. All things
were made by him ; and without him was not any
thing made that was made. In him was life, and
the life was the light of men. And the light
shineth in darkness, and the darkness compre-
hended it not. There was a man sent from God,
whose name was John. The same came for a

witness, to bear witness of the light, that all men through him might believe.   He was not that light, but was sent to bear witness of that light. That was the true light, which lighteth every man that cometh into the world.   He was in the world, and the world was made by him, and the world knew him not.   He came unto his own, and his own received him not.   But as many as received him, to them gave he power to become the sons of God, even to them that believe on his Name: which were born, not of blood, nor of the will of the flesh, nor of the will of man, but of God.   *(Here genuflect.)*   And the Word was made flesh, and dwelt among us (and we beheld his glory, the glory as of the only-begotten of the Father) full of grace and truth.

℟. Thanks be to God.

And finally he shall bless the Child, saying :

THE BLESSING of God Almighty, the Father, the S ✠ on, and the Holy Ghost, descend upon thee, and remain with thee alway.   ℟. Amen.

Then he sprinkles him with holy Water.

COMMENDATION OF A SOUL

The Parish Priest, vested in surplice and violet stole, with one Clerk, if he may be had, carrying a vessel of holy Water, enters the place and says:

℣. **Peace be to this house.**
℟. **And to all that dwell in it.**

In the sick room the Priest, when aspersing, says:—

THOU shalt purge me, O Lord, with hyssop, and I shall be clean: thou shalt wash me and I shall be whiter than snow.

2. *Then he gives the image of our Saviour crucified to the sick person to kiss, and by effectual words lifts him up to hope of eternal salvation, and sets the image before him, that, looking upon it, he may receive hope of salvation.*

3. *Then, a candle being lighted, he kneels and with all present he devoutly recites the short Litanies in this manner:*

> Lord, have mercy on *him*.
> Christ, have mercy on *him*.
> Lord, have mercy on *him*.

HOLY Mary, pray for *him*.
All holy Angels and Archangels, pray for *him*.
Holy Abel, pray.
All ye choirs of the Just, pray.
Holy Abraham, pray.
Holy John Baptist, pray.

Holy Joseph, pray.
All holy Patriarchs and Prophets, pray for *him*.
Holy Peter, pray.
Holy Paul, pray.
Holy Andrew, pray.
Holy John, pray.
All holy Apostles and Evangelists, pray.
All holy Disciples of the Lord, pray.
All holy Innocents, pray.
Holy Stephen, pray.
Holy Laurence, pray.
All holy Martyrs, pray.
Holy Silvester, pray.
Holy Gregory, pray.
Holy Augustine, pray.
All holy Bishops and Confessors, pray.
Holy Benedict, pray.
Holy Francis, pray.
Holy Camillus, pray.
Holy John of God, pray.
All ye holy Monks and Hermits, pray.
Holy Mary Magdalen, pray.
Holy Lucy, pray.
All holy Virgins and Widows, pray for *him*.
All ye Saints of God, both men and women,
     Intercede for *him*.
Be merciful,
     Spare *him*, O Lord.
Be merciful,
     Deliver *him*, O Lord.
Be merciful,
     Deliver *him*, O Lord.

From thy wrath, deliver *him,* O Lord.
From the peril of death, deliver.
From an evil death, deliver.
From the pains of hell, deliver.
From all evil, deliver.
From the power of the devil, deliver.
By thy Nativity, deliver.
By thy Cross and Passion, deliver.
By thy Death and Burial, deliver.
By thy glorious Resurrection, deliver.
By thy wondrous Ascension, deliver.
By the grace of the Holy Ghost
                    the Paraclete, deliver.
In the day of Judgment, deliver.
We sinners, beseech thee, hear us.
That thou wouldest spare *him,*
                    we beseech thee, hear us.
        Lord, have mercy on *him.*
        Christ, have mercy on *him.*
        Lord, have mercy on *him.*

4. *Then, while the soul is troubled in the agony of its passing, the following Prayers are said:*

PRAYER. *Proficiscere.*

GO forth, Christian soul, from this world, in the name of God the omnipotent Father, who created thee : in the name of Jesus Christ, Son of the living God, who suffered for thee : in the name of the Holy Spirit, who hath been poured out on thee : in the name of the glorious and holy Virgin Mary, Mother of God: in the name of blessed Joseph, illustrious Spouse of the same

Virgin : in the name of Angels and Archangels :
in the name of Thrones and Dominations : in the
name of Princedoms and of Powers : in the name
of Virtues, Cherubim and Seraphim : in the name
of Patriarchs and Prophets : in the name of holy
Apostles and Evangelists : in the name of holy
Martyrs and Confessors: in the name of holy
Monks and Hermits: in the name of holy
Virgins, and all Saints of God, both men and
women. May thy place today be found in peace,
and thy dwelling in holy Sion. Through the same
Christ, our Lord. ℟. Amen.

PRAYER.

O MERCIFUL God, O gracious God, O God,
who according to the multitude of thy mercies
dost blot out the sins of them that repent, and by
pardon and remission dost do away the guilt of
their former offences : look mercifully on this thy
servant N. (this thy handmaid N.), and graciously
hearken unto *him,* who by sincere confession doth
seek remission of all *his* sins. Renew in *him,* most
loving Father, whatsoever hath been corrupted by
earthly frailty, or decayed by the fraud of the devil :
and join this member, which thou hast redeemed,
to the unity of the body of the Church. Have
mercy, O Lord upon his groaning, have mercy on
his tears: and forasmuch as *he* putteth *his* whole
trust in thy mercy admit *him* to the Sacrament of
thy reconciliation. Through Christ, our Lord.
℟. Amen.

Note.—Any or all of the following forms of devotion may be used, as time may permit.

I COMMEND thee, dearest brother (dearest sister), to almighty God, and commit thee to his care, whose creature thou art ; that when thou shalt have paid the debt of all mankind by death, thou mayest return to thy Maker, who formed thee out of the dust of the earth.

When, therefore, thy soul shall depart from the body, may the shining company of the Angels meet thee : may the council of the Apostles draw near to thee : may the triumphant army of white-robed Martyrs come to meet thee : may the glorious band of Confessors, crowned with lilies, encompass thee : may the choir of joyful Virgins receive thee : and may an embrace of blessed repose enfold thee in the bosom of the Patriarchs: may Saint Joseph, the most loving Patron of the dying, lift thee up to great hope : may the holy Virgin Mary, Mother of God, graciously turn her eyes toward thee : may the face of Jesus Christ appear to thee gentle and joyful, and may he give thee a place among those who stand before him for ever.

Mayest thou never know the horror of darkness, nor the flames of hell, nor the bitter pains of eternal death. May the most wicked Satan, with his followers give way before thee : may he tremble at thy coming in the company of Angels, and flee away into the confusion of everlasting night. Let God arise, and let his enemies be scattered : let them also that hate him flee before him. Like as the smoke vanisheth, so shalt thou drive them away : and like as wax melteth at the fire, so let the ungodly perish at the presence of God : but let the righteous be glad and rejoice before God. May all the legions of hell be confounded and put to shame, and may the ministers of Satan not dare to stop thee in thy way.

May Christ, who was crucified for thee, deliver thee from torment. May Christ, who vouchsafed to die for thee, deliver thee from eternal death. May Christ, the Son of the living God, place thee in the ever-verdant pastures of his paradise : and may he, the true Shepherd number thee among his sheep. May he absolve thee from all thy sins, and place thee at his right hand, in the portion of his elect. Mayest thou behold thy Redeemer face to face, and standing alway in his presence, gaze with happy eyes on the open vision of truth. And thus placed amongst the ranks of the Blessed, mayest thou enjoy the sweetness of the contemplation of God for ever and ever. ℟. Amen.

PRAYER.

RECEIVE, O Lord, thy servant (handmaid), into the place of salvation, for which *he* hopeth through thy mercy. ℟. Amen.

Deliver, O Lord, the soul of thy servant (handmaid), from all the dangers of hell, and from the bonds of punishment, and from all tribulations. ℟. Amen.

Deliver, O Lord, the soul of thy servant (handmaid), as thou didst deliver Enoch and Elias from the common death of the world. ℟. Amen.

Deliver, O Lord, the soul of thy servant (handmand), as thou didst deliver Noe from the flood. ℟. Amen.

Deliver, O Lord, the soul of thy servant (handmaid), as thou didst deliver Abraham from Ur of the Chaldees. ℟. Amen.

Deliver, O Lord, the soul of thy servant (handmaid), as thou didst deliver Job from his afflictions. ℟. Amen.

Deliver, O Lord, the soul of thy servant (handmaid), as thou didst deliver Isaac from the sacrifice, and from the hand of his father Abraham. ℟. Amen.

Deliver, O Lord, the soul of thy servant (handmaid), as thou didst deliver Lot from Sodom and from the flame of fire. ℟. Amen.

Deliver, O Lord, the soul of thy servant (handmaid), as thou didst deliver Moses from the hand of Pharaoh, king of the Egyptians. ℟ Amen.

Deliver, O Lord, the soul of thy servant (handmaid), as thou didst deliver Daniel from the den of lions. ℟. Amen.

Deliver, O Lord, the soul of thy servant (handmaid), as thou didst deliver the three children from the burning fiery furnace, and from the hand of the unjust king. ℟. Amen.

Deliver, O Lord, the soul of thy servant (handmaid), as thou didst deliver Susanna from false accusation. ℟. Amen.

Deliver, O Lord, the soul of thy servant (handmaid), as thou didst deliver David from the hand of King Saul, and from the hand of Golia. R̦. Amen.

Deliver, O Lord, the soul of thy servant (handmaid), as thou didst deliver Peter and Paul from prison. R̦. Amen.

And as thou didst deliver the most blessed Thecla, thy Virgin and Martyr, from three most cruel torments, so vouchsafe to deliver the soul of this thy servant (handmaid), and make *him* to rejoice with thee in heavenly felicity. R̦. Amen.

PRAYER.

WE commend to thee, O Lord, the soul of thy servant N. (handmaid N.), and we beseech thee, O Lord Jesu Christ, Saviour of the world, that thou, who for *his* sake didst of thy mercy come down to earth, wouldest not refuse *him* a place in the bosom of thy Patriarchs. Acknowledge, O Lord, thy creature not made by strange gods, but by thee the only living and true God : for there is none other God beside thee, nor any works like unto thy works.

Make *his* soul, O Lord, to rejoice in thy presence, and remember not *his* old sins and excesses which have been provoked by the violence of evil desire. For though *he* hath sinned, yet hath *he* not denied the Father, the Son and the Holy Ghost, but hath believed, and hath had a zeal for God within himself, and hath faithfully adored God, who made all things.

PRAYER.

Remember not, O Lord, we beseech thee, the sins of *his* youth and *his* ignorances : but, according to thy great mercy, be mindful of *him* in the brightness of thy glory.   Let the heavens be opened to *him,* let the Angels rejoice with *him*.   Receive thy servant (handmaid), O Lord, into thy kingdom.

Let Saint Michael, the Archangel of God, who merited the princedom of the heavenly host, receive *him*.   Let the holy Angels of God come forth to meet *him* and lead *him* to the heavenly city Jerusalem.   Let blessed Peter, the Apostle to whom by God were given the keys of the kingdom of heaven, receive *him*. Let Saint Paul, the Apostle, who was counted worthy to be a vessel of election, assist *him.*   Let Saint John the chosen Apostle of God, to whom were revealed the secrets of heaven, intercede for *him*.   Let all the holy Apostles, to whom was given by the Lord the power of binding and loosing, pray for *him.*

Let all the Saints and Elect of God, who in this world have suffered torments for the name of Christ, intercede for *him* : that, loosed from the bonds of the flesh, *he* may be worthy to attain unto the glory of the heavenly kingdom, through the gift of our Lord Jesus Christ : Who, with the Father and the Holy Ghost, liveth and reigneth for ever and ever.   ℞. Amen.

PRAYER.

MAY the most merciful Virgin Mary, Mother of God, who is a most kind comforter of the afflicted, commend the spirit of N . . . the servant

H

(handmaid) of God, to her Son, that by her motherly intercession *he* may not fear the terrors of death ; but may enter rejoicing, in her company, into the mansion of that heavenly country which *his* soul desireth. ℞. Amen.

PRAYER.

O HOLY JOSEPH, Patron of the dying, to thee I flee ; to thee, at whose blessed passing, Jesus and Mary stood by, keeping watch, by this two-fold and most dear pledge, I earnestly commend the soul of this servant (handmaid) N., now labouring in its last agony ; that through thy protection it may be delivered from the snares of the devil and from eternal death, and may be worthy to attain unto everlasting joys. Through the same Christ, our Lord. ℞. Amen.

If the soul still lingers, there may be read this Gospel: (John 17, 1-26), *and*:

The Passion of our Lord Jesus Christ according to John. (John 18 and 19).

A PLEADING OF THE PASSION IN THE NAME OF THE SICK PERSON.

℣. We adore thee, O Christ, and we bless thee.

℞. Because by thy holy cross thou hast redeemed the world.

O GOD, who, for the redemption of the world didst deign to be born, to be circumcised, to be rejected by the Jews, and betrayed by the traitor Judas with a kiss, to be bound with chains, and led like an innocent lamb to the slaughter ; to be ignominiously brought before Annas, Caiaphas, Pilate, and Herod ; to be accused by false witnesses; to be vexed with scourges and reproaches ; to be spit upon, to be crowned with thorns, to be buffeted, to be smitten with a reed, to be blindfolded, to be stripped of thy garments, to be nailed to a Cross, to be lifted up thereon, to be numbered among thieves ; to be made to drink of gall and vinegar, and to be pierced with a spear :

Do thou, O Lord, by these thy most holy sufferings, which I unworthy contemplate, and by thy holy Cross and death, deliver thy servant (handmaid) from the pains of hell, and vouchsafe to lead *him* whither thou didst lead the thief who was crucified with thee, Who livest and reignest with the Father and the Holy Spirit, world without end. ꝶ. Amen.

Then may be said Psalms 118 Confitemini Domino, *and* 119, *vv.* 1-32, Beati immaculati.

THREE DEVOUT AND PROFITABLE PLEADINGS.

Kyrie, eléison.
Christe, eléison.
Kyrie, eléison.

Our Father.   Hail Mary.

PRAYER.

O LORD Jesu Christ, I beseech thee, by thy most holy agony, and the prayer which thou didst offer for us on the Mount of Olives, when thy sweat was, as it were, drops of blood falling upon the earth : that thou wouldest vouchsafe to offer to God the Father almighty, for all the sins of this thy servant, N. (handmaid N.), the bloody sweat, which in thine exceeding sorrow even unto death, thou didst abundantly shed for us. And deliver *him* in this hour of *his* death, from all the anguish and punishment which for *his* sins *he* fears *he* has deserved: Who livest and reignest with the same Father and the Holy Ghost, God, world without end. ℟. Amen.

> Kyrie, eléison.
> Christe, eléison.
> Kyrie, eléison.

Our Father.   Hail Mary.

PRAYER.

O LORD Jesu Christ, who for us didst vouchsafe to die upon the Cross; I beseech thee that thou wouldest vouchsafe to offer and present to God the Father almighty, for the soul of this thy servant, N. (handmaid N.), all the bitterness of thy Passion and of thy sufferings, which thou didst endure on the Cross for us miserable sinners, especially in that hour when thy most holy soul went forth from thy most holy body. And deliver *him* in this hour of *his* death, from all the suffering and punishment which for *his* sins *he* fears *he* has deserved: Who livest and reignest with the same Father and the Holy Ghost, God, world without end. ℟. Amen.

> Kyrie, eléison.
> Christe, eléison.
> Kyrie, eléison.

Our Father.   Hail Mary.

PRAYER.

O LORD Jesu Christ, who by the mouth of the Prophet hast said : I have loved thee with an everlasting love, and therefore with loving kindness have I drawn thee : I beseech thee, by that same love which drew thee down from heaven to earth to endure all thy bitter sufferings, to offer and present them before God the Father almighty, for the soul of this thy servant N. (handmaid N.), and deliver *him* from all the suffering and punishment which for *his* sins *he* fears *he* has deserved. And save *his* soul in this hour of *his* departure. Open to *him* the gate of life, and make *him* to rejoice with thy Saints in everlasting glory.

And do thou also, O most loving Lord Jesu Christ, who hast redeemed us by thy most precious blood, have mercy upon the soul of this thy servant (handmaid), and vouchsafe to lead it to the eververdant and pleasant land of Paradise that *he,* who can nevermore be separated from thee and thine elect, may live to thee in perfect love : Who livest and reignest with the same Father and the Holy Ghost, God, world without end. ℞. Amen.

WHEN THE SOUL IS ABOUT TO DEPART.

Ejaculations that may be oft repeated :—

JESU, JESU, JESU.

Into Thy hands, O Lord, I commend my spirit.
O Lord Jesu Christ, receive my spirit.
Holy Mary, pray for me.

Mary, mother of grace, mother of mercy, do thou protect me from the enemy, and receive me in the hour of death.

Holy Joseph, pray for me.

Holy Joseph, with the blessed Virgin thy Spouse, open unto me the bosom of divine mercy.

Jesu, Mary, Joseph, I give you my heart and my soul.

Jesu, Mary, Joseph, be with me in the last agony.

Jesu, Mary, Joseph, in peace may I sleep and take my rest with you.

2. *When the soul has gone forth from the body, the following Responsory shall be said straightway:*

℞. Come to *his* aid, ye Saints of God ; come to meet *him,* ye Angels of the Lord, * Receiving *his* soul, * Offering it in the sight of the Most High.

℣. May Christ receive thee, who hath called thee, and may the Angels lead thee to Abraham's bosom.

℞. Receiving *his* soul, * Offering it in the sight of the Most High.

℣. Rest eternal grant unto *him,* O Lord, and let light perpetual shine upon *him.*

* Offering it in the sight of the Most High.

Kyrie, eléison.
Christe, eléison.
Kyrie, eléison.

Our Father (secretly).

℣. And lead us not into temptation.

℞. But deliver us from evil.

℣. Rest eternal grant unto *him*, O Lord.
℟. And let light perpetual shine upon *him*.
℣. From the gate of hell.
℟. Deliver *his* soul, O Lord.
℣. May *he* rest in peace.
℟. Amen.
℣. O Lord, hear my prayer.
℟. And let my cry come unto thee.
℣. The Lord be with you.
℟. And with thy spirit.

Let us pray.   *Collect.*

UNTO Thee, O Lord, we commend the soul of thy servant N. (and thy handmaid N.), that being dead to the world *he* may live to thee : and whatsoever sins through the frailty of *his* earthly conversation *he* hath committed, do thou by the pardon of thy most merciful goodness cleanse away. Through Christ, our Lord. ℟. Amen.

3. *If the Departed be a Priest, after his name shall be added the words* : the Priest.

THE ORDER OF FUNERALS

(ACCORDING TO THE WESTERN RITE).

At the appointed time the Clergy and others assemble at the Church, and candles are distributed and lighted. Then the Parish Priest, vested in surplice and black stole, and also, on more solemn occasions, in black cope, shall go to the house of the departed, or, more usually, to the entrance of the Churchyard. A Clerk carrying the Cross goes before (and, on more solemn occasions, there may be two acolytes with candles), accompanied by another bearing holy Water.

2. The Parish Priest, in the house or at the entrance of the Churchyard, sprinkles the body with holy Water, and then says without chant alone:

ANT. If thou, Lord.

PSALM 130. *De profundis.*

OUT of the deep have I called unto thee, O Lord : * Lord, hear my voice.

O let thine ears consider well : * the voice of my complaint.

If thou, Lord, wilt be extreme to mark what is done amiss : * O Lord, who may abide it?

For there is mercy with thee : * therefore shalt thou be feared.

I look for the Lord, my soul doth wait for him : * in his word is my trust.

My soul fleeth unto the Lord : * before the morning watch, I say, before the morning watch.

O Israel, trust in the Lord, for with the Lord there is mercy : * and with him is plenteous redemption.

And he shall redeem Israel : * from all his sins.

Rest eternal : * grant unto *him,* O Lord.

And let light perpetual : * shine upon *him.*

ANT. If thou, Lord, wilt be extreme to mark what is done amiss : O Lord, who may abide it?

If the Funeral is performed for several departed, in this verse and in all versicles and Prayers· the plural number is used, except in the Collect Enter not, *page 125.*

Then the body is borne forth from the house (or Churchyard gate), and the Parish Priest straightway intones the Antiphon :

The bones which have been broken.

The Cantors begin and the Clergy continue alternately :

PSALM 51. *Miserere mei, Deus.*

H AVE mercy upon me, O God, after thy great goodness : * according to the multitude of thy mercies do away mine offences.

Wash me throughly from my wickedness : * and cleanse me from my sin.

For I acknowledge my faults : * and my sin is ever before me.

Against thee only have I sinned, and done this evil in thy sight : * that thou mightest be justified in thy saying, and clear when thou art judged.

Behold, I was shapen in wickedness : * and in sin hath my mother conceived me.

But lo, thou requirest truth in the inward parts : * and shalt make me to understand wisdom secretly.

Thou shalt purge me with hyssop, and I shall be clean : * thou shalt wash me, and I shall be whiter than snow.

Thou shalt make me hear of joy and gladness: * that the bones which thou hast broken may rejoice.

Turn thy face from my sins : * and put out all my misdeeds.

Make me a clean heart, O God : * and renew a right spirit within me.

Cast me not away from thy presence : * and take not thy holy Spirit from me.

O give me the comfort of thy help again : * and stablish me with thy free Spirit.

Then shall I teach thy ways unto the wicked : * and sinners shall be converted unto thee.

Deliver me from blood-guiltiness, O God, thou that art the God of my health : * and my tongue shall sing of thy righteousness.

Thou shalt open my lips, O Lord : * and my mouth shall shew thy praise.

For thou desirest no sacrifice, else would I give it thee : * but thou delightest not in burnt offerings.

The sacrifice of God is a troubled spirit : * a broken and contrite heart, O God, shalt thou not despise.

O be favourable and gracious unto Sion : *
build thou the walls of Jerusalem.

Then shalt thou be pleased with the sacrifice
of righteousness, with the burnt offerings and
oblations : * then shall they offer young bullocks
upon thine altar.

Rest eternal : * grant unto *him,* O Lord.

And let light perpetual : * shine upon *him.*

ANT. The bones which have been broken
shall rejoice unto the Lord.

*If the way be long one or more of the Gradual
Psalms 120-134 may be added, (see page 137.)*

3. *Upon entering the church, the Psalm is dis-
continued and the Antiphon* The Bones *is at once
repeated, and they sing the Responsory, the Cantor
beginning, and the Clergy answering alternatively,
viz.*

Subvenite.

Come to his aid, * ye Saints of God, come to
meet *him,* ye Angels of the Lord : * Receiving *his*
soul : † Offering it in the sight of the Most High.

℣. May Christ receive thee, who hath called
thee: and may the Angels lead thee unto Abraham's
bosom. * Receiving *his* soul : † Offering it in the
sight of the Most High.   ℣. Rest eternal grant
unto *him,* O Lord : and let light perpetual shine
upon *him.* † Offering it in the sight of the Most
High.

4. *The bier is set down in the midst of the
Church, so that the feet of the departed, unless he
be a Priest, are toward the High Altar; but if he be
a Priest, his head is toward the Altar; then candles*

being lighted about the body, straightway the Office of the Dead is said.

[*For B.C.P. opening Anthems and Office see page* 144.]

5. *But if neither the Office nor the Mass is to be performed straightway, then, the Responsory* Come to his aid *having been sung, there shall be said :*

Kyrie, eléison. Christe, eléison. Kyrie, eléison.

Our Father, *secretly as far as :*

℣. And lead us not into temptation.
℟. But deliver us from evil.
℣. From the gate of hell.
℟. Deliver *his* soul, O Lord.
℣. May *he* rest in peace.
℟. Amen.
℣. O Lord, hear my prayer.
℟. And let my cry come unto thee.
℣. The Lord be with you.
℟. And with thy spirit.

Let us pray. *Collect.*

ABSOLVE, we beseech thee, O Lord, the soul of thy servant N. (handmaid N.) from every bond of sin : that in the glory of the resurrection *he* may be raised up amid thy Saints and elect unto newness of life. Through Christ, our Lord. ℟. Amen.

If the departed be a Priest, after his name shall be added the words the Priest.

If neither Mass nor Absolution nor Burial follow immediately, there shall be added :

℣. Rest eternal grant unto *him*, O Lord.
℟. And let light perpetual shine upon *him*.
℣. May *he* rest in peace.
℟. Amen.

6. *While the Office is being said, the Priest with the Ministers makes ready to celebrate solemn Mass for the dead, as on the day of burial in the* ENGLISH MISSAL.

7. *At the end of Mass the Celebrant retires to the Epistle corner, where he takes off his chasuble and maniple, and puts on a black cope. The Subdeacon, between two Acolytes with lighted candles, carries the Cross as in Processions, two other Acolytes preceding them, one with the thurible and incense-boat, the other with the holy-water bason and sprinkler. The Celebrant follows, having first made a reverence to the Altar, with the Deacon on his left. The Subdeacon with the Cross takes his stand at the feet of the bier or catafalque opposite the Altar, between the aforesaid Acolytes holding candles, while the Celebrant stands on the other side at the head of the place between the Altar and the bier, turning a little towards the Epistle corner, so that he looks towards the Subdeacon's Cross; on his left the Deacon and near him the two other Acolytes carrying the thurible and holy Water bason. Then, an Acolyte or Clerk holding the book, the Celebrant says at once the following Collect (no change of number or sex being made, even if it is said for many persons or a woman): [which Collect however is omitted, if the body be not present.]*

ENTER not into judgment with thy servant, O Lord, for in thy sight shall no man living be justified, except thou grant unto him remission of

all his sins.   Therefore, we beseech thee, let not
the sentence of thy judgment fall upon him, whom
the faithful prayer of Christian people commendeth
unto thee : but by the succour of thy grace let him
who while he lived was sealed with the sign of the
Holy Trinity be found worthy to escape the aveng-
ing judgment : Who livest and reignest world
without end.   ℞.   Amen.

8.   *Then the Cantor beginning, the Clergy standing around sing the following Responsory:*

Deliver me, O Lord, * from death eternal in that
fearful day : * When the heavens and the earth
shall be shaken : † When thou shalt come to judge
the world by fire.   ℣. I am in fear and trembling
till the sifting be upon us, and the wrath to come.
* When the heavens and the earth shall be shaken.
℣. O that day, that day of anger, of calamity and
misery, a great day and exceeding bitter. † When
thou shalt come to judge the world by fire.
℣. Rest eternal grant unto them, O Lord : and let
light perpetual shine upon them.

Repeat : ℞.   Deliver me *up to the* ℣.   I am.

9.   *Towards the end of the Responsory the
Celebrant puts incense into the thurible, blessing it
as usual, the Deacon ministering the boat.   The
Responsory ended, a Cantor with the first Choir says:*

Kyrie, eléison.

and the second Choir answers:

Christe, eléison.

Then all together say:

Kyrie, eléison.

10. *Then the Priest says in a loud voice:*

Our Father.

And it is continued secretly by all. Meanwhile the Priest receives the sprinkler from the hand of the Deacon, and makes a reverence to the Altar; the Deacon accompanying him on his right, and holding the fore-edge of the Cope, he goes around the bier sprinkling it with holy Water, thrice on the right side and thrice on the left. When he passes in front of the Cross he bows low, while the Deacon genuflects: afterwards he receives the thurible from the Deacon, and censes the bier in the same manner as he has sprinkled it. Having returned to his first position, the Deacon holding the book, he says with joined hands:

℣. And lead us not into temptation.

℟. But deliver us from evil.

℣. From the gate of hell.

℟. Deliver *his* (her) soul (*their* souls), O Lord.

℣. May (*s*)he (*they*) rest in peace.

℟. Amen.

℣. O Lord, hear my prayer.

℟. And let my cry come unto thee.

℣. The Lord be with you.

℟. And with thy spirit.

Let us pray. *Collect.*

O GOD, whose property is ever to have mercy and to forgive, we humbly entreat thee for the soul of thy servant N. (the Priest), (handmaid N.), which thou hast this day commanded to depart from this world : deliver it not into the hands of the enemy, neither forget it at the last, but command that it be received by thy holy Angels, and brought unto the fatherland of paradise : that forasmuch as (s)*he* hoped and believed in thee, (s)*he* may not undergo the pains of hell, but may obtain everlasting felicity.   Through Christ, our Lord. ℞. **Amen.**

11.   The Collect being ended, the body is borne to the grave, if it is then to be borne.

When the body is not present, in place of the preceding Collect the Celebrant says the following, or any other suitable Collect:

Let us pray.   *Collect.*

A BSOLVE, O Lord, we beseech thee, the soul of thy servant N. (handmaid N., *or* souls of thy servants N. and N.) from every bond of sin : that in the glory of the resurrection he (*or* she *or* they) may be raised up amid thy Saints and elect unto newness of life.   Through Christ, our Lord. ℞.. **Amen.**

(*or on All Souls' Day the Collect O God the Creator, with a shorter ending, as on page* 134.)

Then the Celebrant, making a Cross with his right hand over the bier, says:

℣.   Rest eternal grant unto him (*or* her *or* them), O Lord.

℞.   And let light perpetual shine upon him (*or* her *or* them).

And the Cantors having sung:

℣.   May s(he) (they) rest in peace.
℞.   **Amen.**

The Celebrant, again making a Cross over the bier, says on one note :

℣. May his (her) soul (their souls) and the souls of all the faithful departed through the mercy of God rest in peace.

℟. Amen.

Then all return to the Sacristy (see page 134). But the Verse **May his soul,** *and the Psalm* **De Prufundis** *and the rest on page 134, are not said if the Absolution has been made for all the Departed.*

While the body is borne to the grave, or in the same place, if it be not then borne, the Clerks sing the Antiphon :

In Paradisum.

INTO Paradise * may the Angels lead thee : at thy coming may the Martyrs receive thee, and bring thee into the holy city Jerusalem. May the Choir of Angels receive thee, and with Lazarus, once poor, mayest thou have eternal rest.

If the way be long, the recitation of the Gradual Psalms 120-134 may be continued, at the point where they were interrupted.

12. [*When they come to the grave, and if the cemetery has not been consecrated, or if the grave itself has not been previously blessed, and, in any case, if it be masonry-lined, the Priest blesses it, saying :*

Let us pray.   *Collect.*

O GOD, by whose mercy the souls of the faithful are at rest, vouchsafe to ble ✠ ss this grave, and appoint thy holy Angel to guard it : and do thou absolve from every bond of sin the souls of them whose bodies are buried herein : that in thee and with thy Saints they may rejoice everlastingly. Through Christ, our Lord. ℟. Amen.

If the grave is to serve for one person only, there shall be said :

The soul of *him,* whose body is buried herein . . . *he* may rejoice.

13. *The Collect being said, the Priest shall sprinkle with holy Water and then incense the body of the departed and the grave.*

But if the grave be already blessed or the cemetery consecrated, this prayer and the sprinkling and censing of the body and grave are omitted.]

(It is customary according to Western Use to lower the body into the grave during the following Canticle.)

14. *Then, even if the body be not straightway borne to the grave, the Priest shall proceed with the Office, as below, which is never omitted; and shall intone :*

ANT. I am.

SONG OF ZACHARIAS.

Luke 1, 68. *Benedictus.*

B LESSED be the Lord God of Israel : * for he hath visited and redeemed his people :

And hath raised up a mighty salvation for us : * in the house of his servant David.

As he spake by the mouth of his holy prophets : * which have been since the world began :

That we should be saved from our enemies : * and from the hand of all that hate us :

To perform the mercy promised to our fore-fathers : * and to remember his holy covenant.

To perform the oath which he sware to our forefather Abraham : * that he would give us :

That we being delivered out of the hand of our enemies : * might serve him without fear.

In holiness and righteousness before him : * all the days of our life.

And thou, Child, shalt be called the Prophet of the Highest : * for thou shalt go before the face of the Lord to prepare his ways :

To give knowledge of salvation unto his people : * for the remission of their sins :

Through the tender mercy of our God : * whereby the day-spring from on high hath visited us :

To give light to them that sit in darkness, and in the shadow of death : * and to guide our feet into the way of peace.

Rest eternal * grant unto *him,* O Lord.

And let light perpetual * shine upon *him.*

ANT. I am the resurrection and the life : he that believeth in me, though he were dead, yet shall he live : and whosoever liveth and believeth in me shall never die.

Then the Priest says :

Kyrie, eléison.

The Choir continues :

Christe, eléison.
Kyrie, eléison.

Priest : Our Father.

Meanwhile he sprinkles the body without going round.

℣. And lead us not into temptation.
℟. But deliver us from evil.
℣. From the gate of hell.
℟. Deliver *his* soul, O Lord.
℣. May *he* rest in peace.
℟. Amen.
℣. O Lord, hear my prayer.
℟. And let my cry come unto thee.
℣. The Lord be with you.
℟. And with thy spirit.

Let us pray.   *Collect.*

GRANT, we beseech thee, O Lord, this mercy to thy servant (handmaid) departed ; that, forasmuch as *he* desired to do thy will, *he* may not suffer the punishment of *his* misdeeds : that, as true faith joined *him* to the company of the faithful here below, so in heaven thy mercy may number *him* among the angelic choirs. Through Christ, our Lord. ℟. Amen.

Then the Celebrant, making a Cross with his right hand over the bier, says :

℣. Rest eternal grant unto *him,* O Lord.
℟. And let light perpetual shine upon *him.*
℣. May *he* rest in peace.
℟. Amen.

MAY *his* soul, and the souls of all the faithful departed, through the mercy of God, rest in peace. ℟. Amen.

According to custom the Priest may remain and say extra-liturgical prayers:

Let us pray.

GRANT, O Lord, we beseech thee, that whilst we lament the departure of thy servant, we may always remember that we are most certainly to follow *him*. Give us grace to prepare for that last hour by a good and holy life, that we may not be taken unprepared by sudden death ; but may ever be on the watch, that, when thou shalt call, we may go forth to meet the Bridegroom, and enter with him into glory everlasting. Through Jesus Christ, our Lord. *Amen.*

Let us pray.

ALMIGHTY and most merciful Father, who knowest the weakness of our nature, incline thine ear in pity unto thy servants, upon whom thou hast laid the heavy burden of sorrow. Take away out of their hearts the spirit of rebellion and teach them to see thy good and gracious purpose working in all the trials which thou dost send upon them. Grant that they may not languish in fruitless and unavailing grief, nor sorrow as those who have no hope, but through their tears look meekly up to thee, the God of all consolation. Through Jesus Christ, our Lord. *Amen.*

[*For B.C.P. Order of Burial, see page* 149.]

15. *While they return from the grave to the church, or from the church to the sacristy, the Cross going before, the Celebrant begins without chant the*

Antiphon, **If thou O Lord,** *and with the Clergy recites the Psalm,* **De Profundis,** *as above, page* 120.

At the end of the Psalm is added in the plural number :

Rest eternal, etc.

And the whole Antiphon is repeated by all.

Then the Priest in the sacristy, before he puts off the vestments, says the following Prayers (always in the plural number) :

Kyrie, eléison.
Christe, eléison.
Kyrie, eléison.

Our Father, *secretly as far as*

℣. And lead us not into temptation.
℟. But deliver us from evil.
℣. From the gate of hell.
℟. Deliver their souls, O Lord.
℣. May they rest in peace.
℟. Amen.
℣. O Lord, hear my prayer.
℟. And let my cry come unto thee.
℣. The Lord be with you.
℟. And with thy spirit.

Let us pray.   *Collect.*

O GOD, the Creator and Redeemer of the faithful, grant unto the souls of thy servants and handmaids remission of all their sins, that through devout supplications they may obtain the pardon which they have alway desired : Who livest and reignest, world without end. ℟. Amen.

℣. Rest eternal grant unto them, O Lord.

℟. And let light perpetual shine upon them.

℣. May they rest in peace.

℟. Amen.

THE SIMPLEST FORM OF FUNERAL

The Priest, in surplice and black stole, and uncovered, meets the body at the entrance of the Church or Churchyard. He sprinkles it thrice with holy Water, and says the Psalm **De Profundis** *with Antiphon, page* 120. *Then going towards the Altar, he says,* **Come to his aid,** *then* **Our Father, etc.,** *standing at the foot of the body. Then he reads the Absolution and all else as above.*

Or in a Cemetery, if he goes straight from the entrance to the grave, he says the **De Profundis** *as above, at the gate, then on the way says the* **Miserere** *(if there be time) and* **Subvenite ;** *the Absolution,* **In Paradisum** *and the rest at the grave.*

THE RITE OF ABSOLUTION WHEN THE BODY IS NOT PRESENT.

All as on page 125. *But the Prayer* **Enter not** *is omitted, and after the Collect the Versicles* **Rest eternal, etc.,** *are added, as noted (page* 128).

OFFICE OF THE DEAD
AT VESPERS

If this Office immediately follows the bringing of the corpse to the Church and the Responsory **Subvenite, Our Father,** *and* **Hail Mary** *are not said beforehand, but the Office is begun at once with the*

ANT. I will walk before the Lord * in the land of the living.

PSALM 116. *Dilexi, quoniam.*

I AM well pleased, * that the Lord hath heard the voice of my prayer ;

That he hath inclined his ear unto me : * therefore will I call upon him as long as I live.

The snares of death compassed me round about : * and the pains of hell gat hold upon me.

I shall find trouble and heaviness ; and I will call upon the Name of the Lord : * O Lord, I beseech thee, deliver my soul.

Gracious is the Lord, and righteous : * yea, our God is merciful.

The Lord preserveth the simple : * I was in misery, and he helped me.

Turn again then unto thy rest, O my soul : * for the Lord hath rewarded thee.

And why? thou hast delivered my soul from death : * mine eyes from tears, and my feet from falling.

I will walk before the Lord * in the land of the living.

Rest eternal * grant unto them, O Lord.

And let light perpetual * shine upon them.

ANT. I will walk before the Lord in the land of the living.

ANT. Woe is me, O Lord, * that I am constrained to dwell with Mesech.

PSALM 120. *Ad Dominum.*

WHEN I was in trouble I called upon the Lord : * and he heard me.

Deliver my soul, O Lord, from lying lips, * and from a deceitful tongue.

What reward shall be given or done unto thee, thou false tongue? * even mighty and sharp arrows, with hot burning coals.

Woe is me, that I am constrained to dwell with Mesech, * and to have my habitation among the tents of Kedar.

My soul hath long dwelt among them * that are enemies unto peace.

I labour for peace, but when I speak unto them thereof, * they make them ready to battle.

Rest eternal, etc.

ANT. Woe is me, O Lord, that I am constrained to dwell with Mesech.

ANT. The Lord shall preserve thee * from all evil : yea it is even he that shall keep thy soul.

PSALM 121. *Levavi oculos.*

I WILL lift up mine eyes unto the hills, * from whence cometh my help.

My help cometh even from the Lord, * who hath made heaven and earth.

He will not suffer thy foot to be moved : *
and he that keepeth thee will not sleep.

Behold, he that keepeth Israel * shall neither
slumber nor sleep.

The Lord himself is thy keeper, * the Lord is
thy defence upon thy right hand ;

So that the sun shall not burn thee by day : *
neither the moon by night.

The Lord shall preserve thee from all evil : *
yea, it is even he that shall keep thy soul.

The Lord shall preserve thy going out, and thy
coming in : * from this time forth for evermore.

Rest eternal, etc.

ANT. The Lord shall preserve thee from all
evil : yea, it is even he that shall keep thy soul.

ANT. If thou, * Lord, wilt be extreme to
mark what is done amiss : O Lord, who may abide
it?

PSALM 130. *De profundis.*

OUT of the deep have I called unto thee, O Lord;
* Lord, hear my voice.

O let thine ears consider well * the voice of
my complaint.

If thou, Lord, wilt be extreme to mark what
is done amiss : * O Lord, who may abide it?

For there is mercy with thee : * therefore shalt
thou be feared.

I look for the Lord ; my soul doth wait for
him ; * in his word is my trust.

My soul fleeth unto the Lord * before the morning watch, I say, before the morning watch.

O Israel, trust in the Lord, for with the Lord there is mercy, * and with him is plenteous redemption.

And he shall redeem Israel * from all his sins. Rest eternal, etc.

ANT. If thou, * Lord, wilt be extreme to mark what is done amiss : O Lord, who may abide it?

ANT. Despise not, * O Lord, the works of thine own hands.

PSALM 138. *Confitebor tibi.*

I WILL give thanks unto thee, O Lord, with my whole heart : * even before the gods will I sing praise unto thee.

I will worship toward thy holy temple, and praise thy Name, because of thy loving-kindness and truth : * for thou hast magnified thy Name and thy word above all things.

When I called upon thee, thou heardest me : * and enduedst my soul with much strength.

All the kings of the earth shall praise thee, O Lord : * for they have heard the words of thy mouth :

Yea, they shall sing in the ways of the Lord : * that great is the glory of the Lord.

For though the Lord be high, yet hath he respect unto the lowly : * as for the proud, he beholdeth them afar off.

Though I walk in the midst of trouble, yet shalt thou refresh me : * thou shalt stretch forth thy hand upon the furiousness of mine enemies, and thy right hand shall save me.

The Lord shall make good his loving-kindness toward me : * yea, thy mercy, O Lord, endureth for ever : despise not then the works of thine own hands.

Rest eternal, etc.

ANT. Despise not, O Lord, the works of thine own hands.

℣. I heard a voice from heaven saying unto me. ℟. Blessed are the dead which die in the Lord.

ANT. All * that the Father giveth me shall come to me : and him that cometh to me I will in no wise cast out.

SONG OF THE BLESSED VIRGIN MARY.

Magnificat. LUKE 1, 46-55.

MY soul doth magnify the Lord : * and my spirit hath rejoiced in God my Saviour.

For he hath regarded * the lowliness of his handmaiden.

For behold from henceforth * all generations shall call me blessed.

For he that is mighty hath magnified me : * and holy is his Name.

And his mercy is on them that fear him * throughout all generations.

He hath shewed strength with his arm : * he hath scattered the proud in the imagination of their hearts.

He hath put down the mighty from their seat, * and hath exalted the humble and meek.

He hath filled the hungry with good things : * and the rich he hath sent empty away.

He remembering his mercy hath holpen his servant Israel, * as he promised to our forefathers, Abraham and his seed, for ever.

Rest eternal, etc.

ANT. All that the Father giveth me shall come to me : and him that cometh to me I will in no wise cast out.

Then shall be said, kneeling :

Our Father, *secretly as far as* ℣. And lead us not into temptation. ℟. But deliver us from evil.

The following Psalm is not said on All Souls' Day nor on the day of death or burial.

PSALM 146. *Lauda, anima mea.*

PRAISE the Lord, O my soul ; while I live will I praise the Lord : * yea, as long as I have any being, I will sing praises unto my God.

O put not your trust in princes, nor in any child of man, * for there is no help in them.

For when the breath of man goeth forth he shall turn again to his earth : * and then all his thoughts perish.

Blessed is he that hath the God of Jacob for his help, * and whose hope is in the Lord his God ;

Who made heaven and earth, the sea, and all that therein is ; * who keepeth his promise for ever ;

Who helpeth them to right that suffer wrong ; * who feedeth the hungry.

The Lord looseth men out of prison : * the Lord giveth sight to the blind.

The Lord helpeth them that are fallen : * the Lord careth for the righteous.

The Lord careth for the strangers, he defendeth the fatherless and widow : * as for the way of the ungodly, he turneth it upside down.

The Lord thy God, O Sion, shall be King for evermore, * and throughout all generations.

Rest eternal, etc.

℣. From the gate of hell. ℟. Deliver their souls (*or* his *or* her soul), O Lord. ℣. May they (*or* he *or* she) rest in peace. ℟. Amen. ℣. O Lord, hear my prayer. ℟. And let my cry come unto thee. ℣. The Lord be with you. ℟. And with thy spirit.

On the day of death or Burial.

Let us pray. *Collect.*

ABSOLVE, O Lord, we beseech thee, the soul of thy servant N. (handmaid N.), that being dead to the world, *he* may live to thee; and whatsoever through carnal frailness *he* hath committed in *his* earthly conversation, do thou by the pardon of thy most merciful goodness cleanse away. Through . . . in the unity . . . ℟. Amen.

Or Collect **O God whose property,** *page* 127, *but with the longer ending* **Through . . . in the unity,** etc.

For the Departed in general.

Let us pray.   *Collect.*

O GOD, who didst cause thy servants to enjoy
the dignity of Bishops or Priests in the
apostolic ministry : grant, we beseech thee, that
they may evermore be joined unto the fellowship
of the same.

O GOD, the giver of pardon and lover of man's
salvation : we beseech thee of thy mercy to
grant ; that the brethren, kinsfolk, and benefactors of our congregation who have passed out
of this world, may at the intercession of blessed
Mary ever Virgin and of all thy Saints attain unto
the fellowship of eternal blessedness.

(On All Souls' Day this third Collect only).

O GOD, the Creator and Redeemer of all the
faithful : grant unto the souls of thy servants
and handmaids the remission of all their sins ; that
through devout supplications they may obtain the
pardon which they have alway desired : Who
livest and reignest with God the Father . . . in
the unity . . . ℟. Amen.

Then is said (always in the plural) :

℣. Rest eternal grant unto them, O Lord.
℟. And let light perpetual shine upon them.

℣. May they rest in peace. ℟. Amen.

THE BURIAL OF THE DEAD

(ACCORDING TO THE BOOK OF COMMON PRAYER.)

Here is to be noted that the Office ensuing is not to be used for any that die unbaptized, or excommunicate, or have laid violent hands upon themselves.

The Priest and Clerks meeting the Corpse at the entrance of the Churchyard, and going before it, either into the Church, or toward the grave, shall say, or sing:

I AM the resurrection and the life, saith the Lord; he that believeth in me, though he were dead, yet shall he live: and whosoever liveth and believeth in me shall never die. *St. John* xi. 25, 26.

I KNOW that my Redeemer liveth, and that he shall stand at the latter day upon the earth. And though after my skin worms destroy this body, yet in my flesh shall I see God: whom I shall see for myself, and mine eyes shall behold, and not another.

Job xix. 25, 26, 27.

WE brought nothing into this world, and it is certain we can carry nothing out. The Lord gave, and the Lord hath taken away; blessed be the name of the Lord. I *Tim*. vi. 7. *Job* i. 21.

[In the morning, this Office, if said, should immediately precede the Mass.]

After they are come into the Church, shall be read one or both of these Psalms following:

PSALM 39. *Dixi, custodiam.*

I SAID, I will take heed to my ways: that I offend not in my tongue.

I will keep my mouth as it were with a bridle: while the ungodly is in my sight.

I held my tongue, and spake nothing: I kept silence, yea, even from good words; but it was pain and grief to me.

My heart was hot within me, and while I was thus musing the fire kindled: and at the last I spake with my tongue;

Lord, let me know mine end, and the number of my days: that I may be certified how long I have to live.

Behold, thou hast made my days as it were a span long: and mine age is even as nothing in respect of thee; and verily every man living is altogether vanity.

For man walketh in a vain shadow, and disquieteth himself in vain: he heapeth up riches, and cannot tell who shall gather them.

And now, Lord, what is my hope: truly my hope is even in thee.

Deliver me from mine offences: and make me not a rebuke unto the foolish.

I became dumb, and opened not my mouth: for it was thy doing.

Take thy plague away from me: I am even consumed by means of thy heavy hand.

When thou with rebukes dost chasten man for sin, thou dost make his beauty to consume away, like as it were a moth fretting a garment: every man therefore is but vanity.

Hear my prayer, O Lord, and with thine ears consider my calling: hold not thy peace at my tears.

For I am a stranger with thee: and a sojourner, as all my fathers were.

K

O spare me a little, that I may recover my strength: before I go hence, and be no more seen.

Glory be. As it was.

Psalm 90. *Domine, refugium.*

LORD, thou hast been our refuge: from one generation to another.

Before the mountains were brought forth, or ever the earth and the world were made: thou art God from everlasting, and world without end.

Thou turnest man to destruction: again thou sayest, Come again, ye children of men.

For a thousand years in thy sight are but as yesterday: seeing that is past as a watch in the night.

As soon as thou scatterest them, they are even as a sleep: and fade away suddenly like the grass.

In the morning it is green, and groweth up: but in the evening it is cut down, dried up, and withered.

For we consume away in thy displeasure: and are afraid at thy wrathful indignation.

Thou hast set our misdeeds before thee: and our secret sins in the light of thy countenance.

For when thou art angry all our days are gone: we bring our years to an end, as it were a tale that is told.

The days of our age are threescore years and ten; and though men be so strong, that they come to fourscore years: yet is their strength then but labour and sorrow; so soon passeth it away, and we are gone.

But who regardeth the power of thy wrath: for even thereafter as a man feareth, so is thy displeasure.

So teach us to number our days: that we may apply our hearts unto wisdom.

Turn thee again, O Lord, at the last: and be gracious unto thy servants.

O satisfy us with thy mercy, and that soon: so shall we rejoice and be glad all the days of our life.

Comfort us again now after the time that thou hast plagued us: and for the years wherein we have suffered adversity.

Shew thy servants thy work: and their children thy glory.

And the glorious Majesty of the Lord our God be upon us: prosper thou the work of our hands upon us, O prosper thou our handy-work.

Glory be. As it was.

Then shall follow the Lesson taken out of the fifteenth Chapter of the former Epistle of Saint Paul to the Corinthians.

I. Cor. xv. 20.

NOW is Christ risen from the dead, and become the first fruits of them that slept. For since by man came death, by man came also the resurrection of the dead. For as in Adam all die, even so in Christ shall all be made alive. But every man in his own order: Christ the first fruits; afterwards they that are Christ's at his coming. Then cometh the end, when he shall have delivered up the kingdom to God, even the Father; when he shall have put down all rule, and all authority, and power. For he must reign, till he hath put all enemies under his feet. The last enemy that shall be destroyed is death. For he hath put all things under his feet. But when he saith, all things are put under him, it is manifest that he is excepted, which did put all things under him. And when all things shall be subdued unto him, then shall the Son also himself be subject unto him that put all things under him, that God may be all in all. Else what shall they do which are baptized for the dead, if the dead rise not at all? Why are they then baptized for the dead? and why stand we in jeopardy every hour? I protest by your rejoicing, which I have in Christ Jesus our Lord, I die daily. If after the manner of men I have fought with beasts at Ephesus, what advantageth it me, if the dead rise not? Let us eat and drink; for to-morrow we die. Be not deceived: evil communications corrupt good manners. Awake to righteousness and sin not; for some have not the knowledge of God: I speak this to your shame. But some man will say, How are the dead raised up? and with what body do they come? Thou fool, that which thou sowest is not quickened, except it die. And that which thou sowest, thou sowest not that body that shall be, but bare grain, it may chance of wheat, or of some other grain: But God giveth it a body, as it hath pleased him, and to every seed his own body. All flesh is not the same flesh; but there is one kind of flesh of men, another flesh of beasts, another of fishes, and another of birds. There are also celestial bodies, and bodies terrestrial; but the glory of the celestial is one, and the glory of the terrestrial is another. There is one glory of the sun, and another glory of the moon, and another glory of the stars; for one star differeth from another star in glory. So also is the resurrection of the dead: It is sown in corruption; it is raised in incorruption: It is sown in dishonour; it is raised in glory: It is sown in weakness; it is raised in power: It is sown a natural body; it is raised a spiritual body. There is a natural body, and there is a spiritual body. And so it is written, The first man Adam was made a living soul; the last Adam was made a quickening spirit. Howbeit, that was not first which is spiritual, but that which is natural; and afterwards that which is spiritual. The first man is of the earth, earthy: the second man is the Lord from heaven. As is the earthy, such are they that are earthy: and as is the heavenly, such are they also that are heavenly. And as we have borne the image of the earthy, we shall also bear the image of the heavenly. Now this I say, brethren, that flesh and blood cannot inherit the kingdom of God; neither doth corruption inherit incorruption. Behold, I shew you a mystery: We shall not all sleep, but we shall all be changed, in a moment, in the twinkling of an eye, at the last trump, (for the trumpet shall sound,) and the dead shall be raised incorruptible, and we shall be changed. For this corruptible must put on incorruption, and this mortal must put on immortality. So when this corruptible shall have put on incorruption, and this mortal shall have put on immortality; then shall be brought to pass the saying that is written, Death is swallowed up in victory. O death, where is thy sting? O grave, where is thy victory? The sting of death is sin; and the strength of sin is the law. But thanks be to God, which giveth us the victory through our Lord Jesus Christ. Therefore, my beloved brethren, be ye steadfast, unmoveable, always abounding in the work of the Lord, forasmuch as ye know that your labour is not in vain in the Lord.

When they come to the grave, while the Corpse is being made ready to be laid into the earth, the Priest shall say, or the Priest and Clerks shall sing:

M AN that is born of a woman hath but a short time to live, and is full of misery. He cometh up and is cut down like a flower; he fleeth as it were a shadow, and never continueth in one stay.

In the midst of life we are in death : of whom may we seek for succour, but of thee, O Lord, who for our sins art justly displeased?

Yet, O Lord God most holy, O Lord most mighty, O holy and most merciful Saviour, deliver us not into the bitter pains of eternal death.

Thou knowest, Lord, the secrets of our hearts; shut not thy merciful ears to our prayers; but spare us, Lord most holy, O God most mighty, O holy and merciful Saviour, thou most worthy Judge eternal, suffer us not, at our last hour, for any pains of death to fall from thee.

Then, while the earth shall be cast upon the Body by some standing by, the Priest shall say:

FORASMUCH as it hath pleased Almighty God of his great mercy to take unto himself the soul of our dear *brother* here departed, we therefore commit *his* body to the ground; earth to earth, ashes to ashes, dust to dust, in sure and certain hope of the Resurrection to eternal life, through our Lord Jesus Christ; who shall change our vile body that it may be like unto his glorious body, according to the mighty working, whereby he is able to subdue all things to himself.

Then shall be said or sung:

I HEARD a voice from heaven, saying unto me, Write, From henceforth blessed are the dead which die in the Lord; even so saith the Spirit; for they rest from their labours.

Then the Priest shall say:

Lord have mercy upon us.
Christ have mercy upon us.
Lord have mercy upon us.

OUR Father, which art in heaven, Hallowed be thy name. Thy kingdom come. Thy will be done, in earth as it is in heaven. Give us this day our daily bread. And forgive us our trespasses, As we forgive them that trespass against us. And lead us not into temptation; But deliver us from evil. Amen.

Priest.

ALMIGHTY God, with whom do live the spirits of them that depart hence in the Lord, and with whom the souls of the faithful, after they are delivered from the burden of the flesh, are in joy and felicity; we give thee hearty thanks for that it hath pleased thee to deliver this our *brother* out of the miseries of this sinful world; beseeching thee, that it may please thee, of thy gracious goodness, shortly to accomplish the number of thine elect, and to hasten thy kingdom; that we, with all those that are departed in the true faith of thy holy Name, may have our perfect consummation and bliss, both in body and soul, in thine eternal and everlasting glory; Through Jesus Christ our Lord. *Amen.*

The Collect.

O MERCIFUL God, the Father of our Lord Jesus Christ, who is the resurrection and the life; in whom whosoever believeth shall live, though he die; and whosoever liveth and believeth in him, shall not die eternally; who also hath taught us, by his holy Apostle Saint Paul, not to be sorry, as men without hope, for them that sleep in him; We meekly beseech thee, O Father, to raise us from the death of sin unto the life of righteousness; that, when we shall depart this life, we may rest in him, as our hope is this our *brother* doth; and that, at the general Resurrection in the last day, we may be found acceptable in thy sight; and receive that blessing, which thy well beloved Son shall then pronounce to all that love and fear thee, saying. Come ye blessed children of my Father, receive the kingdom prepared for you from the beginning of the world: Grant this, we beseech thee, O merciful Father, through Jesus Christ, our Mediator and Redeemer. *Amen.*

THE grace of our Lord Jesus Christ, and the love of God, and the fellowship of the Holy Ghost, be with us all evermore. *Amen.*

THE BURIAL OF CHILDREN

The following service is to be used at the burial of Children who die before they come to years of discretion (that is, normally, under eight years of age).

At the funeral of such Children the Church bells should be rung joyfully, not tolled as for adults. When a Child who has been baptized, but has not reached the years of discretion, dies, he should be clothed suitably according to age; and a crown of flowers or aromatic and sweet-scented herbs—signifying the integrity and virginity of his body—should be placed upon his head.

The Parish Priest, vested in surplice and white stole, accompanied by a Clerk bearing holy Water, and with others of the Clergy, if any be present, preceded by a Cross borne without its staff, shall come to the place where the dead Child is, and sprinkling the body with holy Water, shall say:

ANT. Blessed be the name of the Lord.

PSALM 113. *Laudate, pueri.*

PRAISE the Lord, ye servants : * O praise the name of the Lord.

Blessed be the name of the Lord : * from this time forth for evermore.

The Lord's name is praised : * from the rising up of the sun unto the going down of the same.

The Lord is high above all heathen : * and his glory above the heavens.

Who is like unto the Lord our God, that hath his dwelling so high : * and yet humbleth himself to behold the things that are in heaven and earth?

He taketh up the simple out of the dust : *
and lifteth the poor out of the mire ;

That he may set him with the princes : * even
with the princes of his people.

He maketh the barren woman to keep house :
* and to be a joyful mother of children.

Glory be.　As it was.

ANT.　Blessed be the name of the Lord :
from this time forth for evermore.

2.　*While the body is being borne to the Church
psalms 119, 1-16; and 17-32 (each part with
Glory be etc.) may be said or sung. But if the Priest
does not go to the house this is omitted and in such
case the sprinkling with holy Water is done at the
Church door and Psalm 113 recited.*

[*For B.C.P. Office see page 144; for another Psalm and Lesson,
see page 161.*]

*If Mass is to be celebrated, a Votive Mass of the
Holy Angels, if the Rubrics permit, may be said,
otherwise Mass of the Day.*

*Then the Priest and Assistants shall stand
around the body, as at the Absolution, and there
shall be said :*

ANT.　He (She) shall receive.

PSALM 24.　*Domini est terra.*

THE earth is the Lord's, and all that therein is :
*the compass of the world, and they that dwell
therein.

For he hath founded it upon the seas : * and
prepared it upon the floods.

Who shall ascend into the hill of the Lord : *
or who shall rise up in his holy place?

Even he that hath clean hands, and a pure
heart : * and that hath not lift up his mind unto
vanity, nor sworn to deceive his neighbour.

He shall receive the blessing from the Lord :
* and righteousness from the God of his salvation.

This is the generation of them that seek him :
* even of them that seek thy face, O Jacob.

Lift up your heads, O ye gates, and be ye lift
up, ye everlasting doors : * and the King of glory
shall come in.

Who is the King of glory : * it is the Lord
strong and mighty, even the Lord mighty in battle.

Lift up your heads, O ye gates, and be ye lift
up, ye everlasting doors : * and the King of glory
shall come in.

Who is the King of glory : * even the Lord of
hosts, he is the King of glory.

Glory be.   As it was

ANT.   He (She) shall receive the blessing
from the Lord, and righteousness from the God of
his (her) salvation : for this is the generation of
them that seek the Lord.

The Priest shall then say:

Kyrie, eléison.

The Choir continues:

Christe, eléison.
Kyrie, eléison.

Our Father *(secretly).*

*Meanwhile he sprinkles the body without going
around.*

℣.   And lead us not into temptation.

℟.   But deliver us from evil.

℣.   For mine innocency's sake thou hast received me.

℟.   And hast set me before thy face for ever.

℣.   The Lord be with you.

℟.   And with thy spirit.

Let us pray.   *Collect.*

ALMIGHTY and most merciful God, who dost grant everlasting life unto all infants who have been regenerated in the font of baptism, as they pass from the world, and that without any merit of their own, as we believe that thou hast done this day unto the soul of this child: grant, we beseech thee, O Lord, through the intercession of blessed Mary ever Virgin and of all thy Saints, that we may serve thee here with clean hearts, and be for ever numbered with the blessed little ones in Paradise.   Through Christ, our Lord. ℟ Amen.

Whilst the body is being borne to the grave, or in the same place, if it be not then borne, the following shall be said or sung:

ANT. Young men.

PSALM 148. *Laudate Dominum.*

O PRAISE the Lord of heaven : * praise him in the height.

Praise him all ye Angels of his : * praise him, all his host.

Praise him, sun and moon: * praise him, all ye stars and light.

Praise him all ye heavens : * and ye waters that are above the heavens.

Let them praise the name of the Lord : * for he spake the word and they were made, he commanded and they were created.

He hath made them fast for ever and ever : * he hath given them a law which shall not be broken.

Praise the Lord upon earth : * ye dragons and all deeps ;

Fire and hail, snow and vapours : * wind and storm, fulfilling his word ;

Mountains and all hills : * fruitful trees and all cedars ;

Beasts and all cattle : * worms and feathered fowls ;

Kings of the earth and all people : * princes and all judges of the world ;

Young men and maidens, old men and children, praise the name of the Lord: * for his name only is excellent, and his praise above heaven and earth.

He shall exalt the horn of his people ; all his saints shall praise him : * even the children of Israel, even the people that serveth him.

Glory be. As it was.

ANT. Young men and maidens, old men and children, praise the name of the Lord.

Kyrie, eléison.
Christe, eléison.
Kyrie, eléison.

Our Father (secretly).

℣.　And lead us not into temptation.

℟.　But deliver us from evil.

℣.　Suffer the little children to come unto me.

℟.　For of such is the kingdom of heaven.

℣.　The Lord be with you.

℟.　And with thy spirit.

Let us pray.　　　　　　　　　　　*Collect.*

ALMIGHTY and everlasting God, the lover of holy purity, who hast this day mercifully deigned to call the soul of this child into the kingdom of heaven : vouchsafe likewise, O Lord, so to deal with us in thy mercy ; that, by the merits of thy most holy Passion and the intercession of blessed Mary ever Virgin and of all thy Saints, thou wouldest make us evermore to rejoice in the same kingdom with all thy Saints and elect. Who livest and reignest, world without end. ℟. Amen.

3.　Then the Priest shall sprinkle the body with holy Water, and cense it, and likewise the grave : afterwards the body shall be buried.

[*For B.C.P. Order of Burial, see page* 149.]

[*For Prayers for the Mourners, see page* 133.]

4.　While they return from the grave to the Church, the following is said :

Song of the Three Children.
Daniel 3. *Benedicite.*

Ant.　Bless ye the Lord.

O ALL ye works of the Lord, bless ye the Lord: * praise him and magnify him for ever.

O ye Angels of the Lord, bless ye the Lord : *
O ye heavens, bless ye the Lord.

O ye waters that be above the firmament, bless
ye the Lord : * O all ye Powers of the Lord, bless
ye the Lord.

O ye sun and moon, bless ye the Lord : * O
ye stars of heaven, bless ye the Lord.

O ye showers and dew, bless ye the Lord : *
O ye winds of God, bless ye the Lord.

O ye fire and heat, bless ye the Lord : * O ye
winter and summer, bless ye the Lord.

O ye dews and frosts, bless ye the Lord : * O
ye frost and cold, bless ye the Lord.

O ye ice and snow, bless ye the Lord : * O ye
nights and days, bless ye the Lord.

O ye light and darkness, bless ye the Lord : *
O ye lightnings and clouds, bless ye the Lord.

O let the earth bless the Lord : * yea, let it
praise him and magnify him for ever.

O ye mountains and hills, bless ye the Lord : *
O all ye green things upon the earth, bless ye the
Lord.

O ye wells, bless ye the Lord : * O ye seas and
floods, bless ye the Lord.

O ye whales, and all that move in the waters,
bless ye the Lord : * O ye fowls of the air, bless ye
the Lord.

O ye beasts and cattle, bless ye the Lord : O
ye children of men, bless ye the Lord.

O let Israel bless the Lord : * praise him and
magnify him for ever.

O ye priests of the Lord, bless ye the Lord : *
O ye servants of the Lord, bless ye the Lord.

O ye spirits and souls of the righteous, bless ye
the Lord : * O ye holy and humble men of heart,
bless ye the Lord.

O Ananias, Azarias, and Misael, bless ye the
Lord : * praise him and magnify him for ever.

Let us bless the Father and the Son with the
Holy Ghost : * let us praise him and magnify him
for ever.

Blessed art thou, O Lord, in the firmament of
heaven : * and worthy to be praised and glorious,
and magnified above all for ever.

      Gloria Patri *is not said.*

ANT. Bless ye the Lord, all ye his elect, keep
a day of gladness, and give thanks unto him.

Then standing before the Altar, the Priest says:

℣. The Lord be with you.
℟. And with thy spirit.

Let us pray.   *Collect.*

O EVERLASTING God, who hast ordained and
constituted the services of Angels and men in
a wonderful order : mercifully grant ; that as thy
holy Angels always do thee service in heaven, so
by thy appointment they may succour and defend
us on earth. Through Christ, our Lord.

℟. Amen.

___

*In the Office of the Book of Common Prayer,
(page 145), on occasions to be approved by the*

Ordinary, the following Psalm and Lesson may, with his consent, be substituted for those there appointed:

PSALM 23, *Dominus regit me.*

THE Lord is my shepherd: therefore can I lack nothing.

He shall feed me in a green pasture: and lead me forth beside the waters of comfort.

He shall convert my soul: and bring me forth in the paths of righteousness, for his name's sake.

Yea, though I walk through the valley of the shadow of death, I will fear no evil: for thou art with me; thy rod and thy staff comfort me.

Thou shalt prepare a table before me against them that trouble me: thou hast anointed my head with oil, and my cup shall be full.

But thy loving-kindness and mercy shall follow me all the days of my life: and I will dwell in the house of the Lord for ever.

Glory be. As it was.

The Lesson.

ST. MARK, x, 13-16.

THEY brought young children to Christ that he should touch them; and his disciples rebuked those that brought them. But when Jesus saw it, he was much displeased, and said unto them, Suffer the little children to come unto me and forbid them not; for of such is the kingdom of God. Verily I say unto you, Whosoever shall not receive the kingdom of God as a little child, he shall not enter therein. And he took them up in his arms, put his hands upon them, and blessed them.

L

THE SACRAMENT OF MATRIMONY

The Parish Priest, or his delegate, who is to celebrate the Marriage, comes to the Church vested in surplice and white stole, accompanied by at least one Clerk likewise vested in surplice, who carries the book and the vessel of holy Water with the sprinkler, and questions the man and the woman in the presence of two or three witnesses concerning their consent to the Marriage.

2. *First the Priest shall ask the bridegroom, who stands on the right of the woman:*

N. Wilt thou take N. here present for thy lawful wife, according to the rite of our holy Mother the Church?

The bridegroom shall answer: **I will.**

Then the Priest shall ask the bride:

N. Wilt thou take N. here present for thy lawful husband, according to the rite of our holy Mother the Church?

The bride shall answer: **I will.**

3. *Then the woman is given away by her father or by her friends; if she has not before been married, she shall have her hand uncovered, but, if she be a widow, covered; and the man shall receive her to keep her in the faith of God and his own, and shall hold her right hand in his right hand; and, taught by the Priest, he shall plight his troth in this manner, saying:*

I, *N.* take thee *N.* to my wedded wife, to have, and to hold, from this day forward, for better, for worse, for richer, for poorer, in sickness and in health, till death do us part; and thereto I plight thee my troth.

Then withdrawing her hand, and again joining it, the woman, taught by the Priest, shall say:

I, *N.* take thee *N.* to my wedded husband, to have, and to hold, from this day forward, for better, for worse, for richer, for poorer, in sickness and in health, till death do us part; and thereto I plight thee my troth.

4. *Having both thus plighted their troth, and having joined their hands, the Priest shall say:*

I join you in Matrimony.   In the name of the Father ✠, and of the Son, and of the Holy Ghost. Amen.

Then he shall sprinkle them with holy Water.

Blessing of the Ring.

5. *Then the bridegroom shall put gold and silver (later to be delivered into the hand of the bride) and the ring upon the salver or book; and the Priest blesses it, saying:*

℣. Our help is in the name of the Lord.

℟. Who hath made heaven and earth.

℣. O Lord, hear my prayer.

℟. And let my cry come unto thee.

℣. The Lord be with you.

℟. And with thy spirit.

Let us pray. *Collect.*

BLE ✠ SS, O Lord, this ring, which we ble ✠ ss in thy name, that she who shall wear it, keeping true faith unto her husband, may abide in thy peace and according to thy will, and ever live in mutual love. Through Christ, our Lord. ℟. Amen.

Then the Priest shall sprinkle the ring with holy Water, in the form of a Cross.

6. *And the bridegroom, taking the ring from the hand of the Priest, gives the gold and silver to the bride, and says:*

With this ring I thee wed : this gold and silver I thee give : with my body I thee worship : and with all my worldly goods I thee endow.

Then the bridegroom places the ring on the left thumb of the hand of the bride, saying:

In the name of the Father: *then on the second finger, saying,* and of the Son : *then on the third finger, saying:* and of the Holy Ghost: *lastly on the fourth finger, saying,* Amen. *And there he leaves the ring.*

7. *These things being done, the Priest adds:*

℣. Stablish the thing, O God, which thou hast wrought in us.

℟. For thy temple's sake at Jerusalem.

Kyrie, eléison. Christe, eléison. Kyrie, eléison.

Our Father.

℣. And lead us not into temptation.

℟. But deliver us from evil.

℣. Save thy servants.

℟. Who put their trust in thee, my God.

℣. Send them help, O Lord, from the sanctuary.

℟. And strengthen them out of Sion.

℣. Be unto them, O Lord, a tower of strength.

℟. From the face of the enemy.

℣. O Lord, hear my prayer.

℟. And let my cry come unto thee.

℣. The Lord be with you.

℟. And with thy spirit.

Let us pray. *Collect.*

LOOK, O Lord, we beseech thee, upon these thy servants : and graciously assist this thine institution, whereby thou hast ordained the propagation of mankind : that they who are joined together by thine authority may by thy assistance be preserved. Through Christ, our Lord. ℟. Amen.

8. *These things being done, if the marriage is to be blessed, the Parish Priest, or his delegate, shall celebrate the Mass for Bridegroom and Bride, as in the* ENGLISH MISSAL, *observing all things, which are there prescribed.*

If one of the parties be not in communion with the Church, it is unlawful to bless the marriage in any manner. Otherwise, if Mass be not said, the following form is used:

NUPTIAL BLESSING

OUTSIDE MASS.

The Priest, turning towards the newly-married persons, says:

PSALM 128. *Beati omnes.*

BLESSED are all they that fear the Lord : * and walk in his ways.

For thou shalt eat the labours of thine hands: * O well is thee, and happy shalt thou be.

Thy wife shall be as the fruitful vine : * upon the walls of thine house.

Thy children like the olive-branches : * round about thy table.

Lo, thus shall the man be blessed : * that feareth the Lord.

The Lord from out of Sion shall so bless thee: * that thou shalt see Jerusalem in prosperity all thy life long.

Yea, that thou shalt see thy children's children: * and peace upon Israel.

Glory be. As it was.

Kyrie, eléison. Christe, eléison. Kyrie, eléison.

Our Father, *secretly as far as:*

℣. And lead us not into temptation.
℞. But deliver us from evil.
℣. O Lord, hear my prayer.
℞. And let my cry come unto thee.
℣. The Lord be with you.
℞. And with thy spirit.

Let us pray.   *Collect.*

BLESS, ✠ O Lord, and look from heaven upon
this union: and as thou didst send thy holy
Angel Raphael to bring peace to Tobias and
Sarah, the daugher of Raguel, so vouchsafe, O
Lord, to send thy blessing upon these two
persons, that they may abide in thy benediction,
continue in thy will, and live in thy love.
Through Christ, our Lord. ℟. Amen.

*Then raising his hands and extending them over
their heads, the minister holding the book, he says:*

The Lord God almighty bless you, and
fulfil his benediction upon you, and may ye see
your children's children even unto the third and
fourth generation, and attain unto the old age
which ye desire. Through Christ, our Lord.
℟. Amen.

*But if the bride, being a widow, has previously
received the nuptial blessing, or if it be the closed
time, i.e., from Advent Sunday to Christmas Day
inclusive, or from Ash Wednesday to Easter Day
inclusive, then the nuptial blessing may not be given,
but in place thereof the following form is used:*

After Psalm 128, and the **Our Father** *and
Versicles as above, there is said in place of the Collect
and Blessing the following:*

Let us pray.   *Collect.*

STRETCH forth, we beseech thee, O Lord, the
right hand of thy heavenly succour on thy
faithful, that they may seek thee with their whole
heart, and obtain those things which they rightly
ask. Through Christ, our Lord. ℟. Amen.

THE FORM OF
SOLEMNIZATION OF MATRIMONY
(ACCORDING TO THE BOOK OF COMMON PRAYER.)

First the Banns of all that are to be married together must be published in the Church three several Sundays, during the time of Morning Service, or of Evening Service, (if there be no Morning Service,) immediately after the second Lesson; the Curate saying after the accustomed manner:

I PUBLISH the Banns of Marriage between N. of —— and N. of ——. If any of you know cause, or just impediment, why these two persons should not be joined together in holy Matrimony, ye are to declare it. This is the first [*second, or third*] time of asking.

And if the persons that are to be married dwell in divers Parishes, the Banns must be asked in both Parishes; and the Curate of the one Parish shall not solemnize Matrimony betwixt them, without a Certificate of the Banns being thrice asked, from the Curate of the other Parish.

At the day and time appointed for solemnization of Matrimony, the persons to be married shall come into the body of the Church with their friends and neighbours; and there standing together, the Man on the right hand, and the Woman on the left, the Priest shall say:

D EARLY beloved, we are gathered together here in the sight of God, and in the face of this congregation, to join together this Man and this Woman in holy Matrimony; which is an honourable estate, instituted of God in the time of man's innocency, signifying unto us the mystical union that is betwixt Christ and his Church; which holy estate Christ adorned and beautified with his presence, and first miracle that he wrought, in Cana of Galilee; and is commended of Saint Paul to be honourable among all men, and therefore is not by any to be enterprised, nor taken in hand, unadvisedly, lightly, or wantonly, to satisfy men's carnal lusts and appetites, like brute beasts that have no understanding; but reverently, discreetly, advisedly soberly, and in the fear of God; duly considering the causes for which Matrimony was ordained.

First, It was ordained for the procreation of children, to be brought up in the fear and nurture of the Lord, and to the praise of his holy Name.

Secondly, It was ordained for a remedy against sin, and to avoid fornication; that such persons as have not the gift of continency might marry, and keep themselves undefiled members of Christ's body.

Thirdly, It was ordained for the mutual society, help, and comfort, that the one ought to have of the other, both in prosperity and adversity. Into which holy estate these two persons present come now to be joined. Therefore if any man can shew any just cause, why they may not lawfully be joined together, let him now speak, or else hereafter for ever hold his peace.

And also, speaking unto the persons that shall be married, he shall say:

I REQUIRE and charge you both, as ye will answer at the dreadful day of judgment when the secrets of all hearts shall be disclosed, that if either of you know any impediment, why ye may not be lawfully joined together in Matrimony, ye do now confess it.

For be ye well assured, that so many as are coupled together otherwise than God's Word doth allow are not joined together by God; neither is their Matrimony lawful.

At which day of Marriage, if any man do allege and declare any impediment, why they may not be coupled together in Matrimony, by God's Law, or the Laws of this Realm; and will be bound, and sufficient sureties with him, to the parties; or else put in a Caution (to the full value of such charges as the persons to be married do thereby sustain) to prove his allegation: then the solemnization must be deferred, until such time as the truth be tried.

If no impediment be alleged, then shall the Curate say unto the Man:

N. . . ., WILT thou have this Woman to thy wedded wife, to live together after God's ordinance in the holy estate of Matrimony? Wilt thou love her, comfort her, honour, and keep her in sickness and in health; and, forsaking all other, keep thee only unto her, so long as ye both shall live?

The Man shall answer,

I will.

Then shall the Priest say unto the Woman,

N. . . ., WILT thou have this Man to thy wedded husband, to live together after God's ordinance in the holy estate of Matrimony? Wilt thou obey him, and serve him, love, honour, and keep him in sickness and in health; and, forsaking all other, keep thee only unto him, so long as ye both shall live?

The Woman shall answer,

I will.

Then shall the Minister say :

Who giveth this Woman to be married to this Man?

Then shall they give their troth to each other in this manner.

The Minister, receiving the Woman at her father's or friend's hands, shall cause the Man with his right hand to take the Woman by her right hand, and to say after him as followeth.

I N. take thee N. to my wedded wife, to have and to hold from this day forward, for better for worse, for richer, for poorer, in sickness and in health, to love and to cherish, till death us do part, according to God's holy ordinance; and thereto I plight thee my troth.

Then shall they loose their hands; and the Woman, with her right hand taking the Man by his right hand shall likewise say after the Minister,

I N. take thee N. to my wedded husband, to have and to hold from this day forward, for better for worse, for richer, for poorer, in sickness and in health, to love, cherish, and to obey, till death us do part, according to God's holy ordinance; and thereto I give thee my troth.

[*For the Blessing of the Ring, see page* 163.]

Then shall they again loose their hands; and the Man shall give unto the Woman a Ring, laying the same upon the book with the accustomed duty to the Priest and Clerk. And the Priest, taking the Ring, shall deliver it unto the Man, to put it upon the fourth finger of the Woman's left hand. And the Man holding the Ring there, and taught by the Priest, shall say,

WITH this Ring I thee wed, with my body I thee worship, and with all my worldly goods I thee endow: in the Name of the Father, and of the Son, and of the Holy Ghost. Amen.

Then the Man leaving the Ring upon the fourth finger of the Woman's left hand, they shall both kneel down; and the Minister shall say,

Let us pray.

O ETERNAL God, Creator and Preserver of all mankind, Giver of all spiritual grace, the Author of everlasting life; Send thy blessing upon these thy servants, this man and this woman, whom we bless in thy Name; that, as Isaac and Rebecca lived faithfully together, so these persons may surely perform and keep the vow and covenant betwixt them made, (whereof this Ring given and received is a token and pledge,) and may ever remain in perfect love and peace together, and live according to thy laws; through Jesus Christ our Lord. *Amen.*

Then shall the Priest join their right hands together, and say,

Those whom God hath joined together let no man put asunder.

Then shall the Minister speak unto the people.

FORASMUCH as *N.* and *N.* have consented together in holy wedlock, and have witnessed the same before God and this company, and thereto have given and pledged their troth either to other, and have declared the same by giving and receiving of a Ring, and by joining of hands; I pronounce that they be Man and Wife together, In the Name of the Father, and of the Son, and of the Holy Ghost. Amen.

And the Minister shall add this Blessing:

GOD the Father, God the Son, God the Holy Ghost, bless, preserve, and keep you; the Lord mercifully with his favour look upon you; and so fill you with all spiritual benediction and grace, that ye may so live together in this life, that in the world to come ye may have life everlasting.   Amen.

Then the Minister or Clerks, going to the Lord's Table, shall say or sing this Psalm following:

Psalm 128.   *Beati omnes.*

BLESSED are all they that fear the Lord: and walk in his ways.

For thou shalt eat the labour of thine hands: O well is thee, and happy shalt thou be.

Thy wife shall be as the fruitful vine: upon the walls of thine house;

Thy children like the olive-branches: round about thy table.

Lo, thus shall the man be blessed: that feareth the Lord.

The Lord from out of Sion shall so bless thee: that thou shalt see Jesusalem in prosperity all thy life long;

Yea, that thou shalt see thy children's children: and peace upon Israel.

Glory be to the Father, and to the Son: and to the Holy Ghost;

As it was in the beginning, is now, and ever shall be: world without end.   Amen.

Or this Psalm.

Psalm 67.   *Deus misereatur.*

GOD be merciful unto us, and bless us: and shew us the light of his countenance, and be merciful unto us.

That thy way may be known upon earth: thy saving health among all nations.

Let the people praise thee, O God: yea, let all the people praise thee.

O let the nations rejoice and be glad: for thou shalt judge the folk righteously, and govern the nations upon earth.

Let the people praise thee, O God: yea, let all the people praise thee.

Then shall the earth bring forth her increase: and God, even our own God, shall give us his blessing.

God shall bless us: and all the ends of the world shall fear him.

Glory be to the Father, and to the Son: and to the Holy Ghost;

As it was in the beginning, is now, and ever shall be: world without end. Amen.

The Psalm ended, and the Man and the Woman kneeling before the Lord's Table, the Priest standing at the Table, and turning his face towards them, shall say:

Lord, have mercy upon us.

Answer. Christ, have mercy upon us.

Minister. Lord, have mercy upon us.

OUR Father, which art in heaven, Hallowed be thy Name. Thy kingdom come. Thy will be done, in earth as it is in heaven. Give us this day our daily bread. And forgive us our trespasses, As we forgive them that trespass against us, And lead us not into temptation; But deliver us from evil. Amen.

Minister. O Lord, save thy servant and thy handmaid;

Answer. Who put their trust in thee.

Minister.   O Lord, send them help from thy holy place;

Answer.   And evermore defend them.

Minister.   Be unto them a tower of strength,

Answer.   From the face of their enemy.

Minister.   O Lord, hear our prayer.

Answer.   And let our cry come unto thee.

Minister:

O GOD of Abraham, God of Isaac, God of Jacob, bless these thy servants, and sow the seed of eternal life in their hearts; that whatsoever in thy holy Word they shall profitably learn, they may in deed fulfil the same. Look, O Lord, mercifully upon them from heaven, and bless them. And as thou didst send thy blessing upon Abraham and Sarah, to their great comfort, so vouchsafe to send thy blessing upon these thy servants; that they obeying thy will, and alway being in safety under thy protection, may abide in thy love unto their lives' end; through Jesus Christ our Lord. *Amen.*

This Prayer next following shall be omitted, where the Woman is past child-bearing.

O MERCIFUL Lord, and heavenly Father, by whose gracious gift mankind is increased; We beseech thee, assist with thy blessing these two persons, that they may both be fruitful in procreation of children, and also live together so long in godly love and honesty, that they may see their children christianly and virtuously brought up, to thy praise and honour; through Jesus Christ our Lord. *Amen.*

O GOD, who by thy mighty power hast made all things of nothing; who also (after other things set in order) didst appoint, that out of man (created after thine own image and similitude) woman should take her beginning; and, knitting them together, didst teach that it should never be lawful to put asunder those whom thou by Matrimony hadst made one: O God, who hast consecrated the state of Matrimony to such an excellent mystery, that in it is signified and represented the spiritual marriage and unity betwixt Christ and his Church; Look mercifully upon these thy servants, that both this man may love his wife, according to thy Word, (as Christ did love his spouse the Church, who gave himself for it, loving and cherishing it even as his own flesh,) and also that this woman may be loving and amiable, faithful and obedient to her husband; and in all quietness, sobriety, and peace, be a follower of holy and godly matrons. O Lord, bless them both,, and grant them to inherit thy everlasting kingdom; through Jesus Christ our Lord. *Amen.*

Then shall the Priest say:

A LMIGHTY God, who at the beginning did create our first parents, Adam and Eve, and did sanctify and join them together in marriage; Pour upon you the riches of his grace, sanctify and bless you, that ye may please him both in body and soul, and live together in holy love unto your lives' end. *Amen.*

After which, if there be no Sermon declaring the duties of Man and Wife, the Minister shall read as followeth.

A LL ye that are married, or that intend to take the holy estate of Matrimony upon you, hear what the holy Scripture doth say as touching the duty of husbands towards their wives, and wives towards their husbands.

Saint Paul, in his Epistle to the Ephesians, the fifth Chapter, doth give this commandment to all married men; Husbands, love your wives, even as Christ also loved the Church, and gave himself for it, that he might sanctify and cleanse it with the washing of water, by the Word; that he might present it to himself a glorious Church, not having spot, or wrinkle, or any such thing; but that it should be holy, and without blemish. So ought men to love their wives as their own bodies. He that loveth his wife loveth himself: for no man ever yet hated his own flesh, but nourisheth and cherisheth it, even as the Lord the Church: for we are members of his body, of his flesh, and of his bones. For this cause shall a man leave his father and mother, and shall be joined unto his wife; and they two shall be one flesh. This is a great mystery; but I speak concerning Christ and the Church. Nevertheless, let every one of you in particular so love his wife, even as himself.

Likewise the same Saint Paul, writing to the Colossians, speaketh thus to all men that are married; Husbands, love your wives, and be not bitter against them.

Hear also what Saint Peter, the Apostle of Christ, who was himself a married man, saith unto them that are married; Ye husbands, dwell with your wives according to knowledge; giving honour unto the wife, as unto the weaker vessel, and as being heirs together of the grace of life, that your prayers be not hindered.

Hitherto ye have heard the duty of the husband toward the wife. Now likewise, ye wives, hear and learn your duties toward your husbands, even as it is plainly set forth in Holy Scripture.

M

Saint Paul, in the aforenamed Epistle to the Ephesians, teacheth you thus; Wives, submit yourselves unto your own husbands, as unto the Lord. For the husband is the head of the wife, even as Christ is the head of the Church: and he is the Saviour of the body. Therefore as the Church is subject unto Christ, so let the wives be to their own husbands in every thing. And again he saith, Let the wife see that she reverence her husband.

And in his Epistle to the Colossians, Saint Paul giveth you this short lesson; Wives, submit yourselves unto you own husbands, as it is fit in the Lord.

Saint Peter also doth instruct you very well, thus saying; Ye wives, be in subjection to you own husbands; that, if any obey not the Word, they also may without the Word be won by the conversation·of the wives; while they behold your chaste conversation coupled with fear. Whose adorning, let it not be that outward adorning of plaiting the hair, and of wearing of gold, or of putting on of apparel; but let it be the hidden man of the heart, in that which is not corruptible; even the ornament of a meek and quiet spirit, which is in the sight of God of great price. For after this manner in the old time the holy women also, who trusted in God, adorned themselves, being in subjection unto their own husbands; even as Sarah obeyed Abraham, calling him lord; whose daughters ye are as long as ye do well, and are not afraid with any amazement.

It is convenient that the newly-married persons should receive the holy Communion at the time of their Marriage, or at the first opportunity after their Marriage.

BLESSING OF A WOMAN IN CHILDBIRTH

℣. Our help is in the name of the Lord.
℞. Who hath made heaven and earth.
℣. O Lord save thy handmaid.
℞. Who putteth her trust in thee.
℣. Be unto her a tower of strength.
℞. From the face of her enemy.
℣. Send her help from thy holy place.
℞. And defend her out of Sion.
℣. O Lord, hear my prayer.
℞. And let my cry come unto thee.
℣. The Lord be with you.
℞. And with thy spirit.

Let us pray. *Collect.*

ALMIGHTY and everlasting God, who hast given unto thy servants grace by the confession of a true faith to acknowledge the glory of the eternal Trinity, and in the power of the Majesty to worship the Unity : we beseech thee; that thou wouldest keep this thine handmaid N . . ., steadfast in this faith, and evermore defend her from all adversities. Through Christ, our Lord. ℞. Amen.

Let us pray. *Collect.*

O LORD God, Creator of all things, strong and mighty, just and merciful, who alone art good and gracious; who didst deliver Israel from every evil, making our fathers thy chosen ones, and didst sanctify them by the hand of thy Spirit; who didst prepare the body and soul of the glorious Virgin Mary that it might be made a worthy dwelling-place for thy Son; who didst fill John the Baptist with the Holy Ghost and didst cause him to rejoice in his mother's womb : receive the sacrifice of a contrite heart, and the fervent desire of thine hand-maid N . . ., who humbly prayeth for the preservation of the offspring which thou hast given her to conceive : keep thy part, and defend her from every sorrow and injury of the malicious enemy : that, by the protecting hand of thy mercy, her offspring may happily come to birth and be preserved in its generation, and may serve thee continually in all things, and be worthy to attain unto everlasting life. Through the same . . . in the unity of the same Holy Ghost. R̸. Amen.

Here the woman shall be sprinkled with holy Water. Then is said:

PSALM 67. *Deus misereatur.*

GOD be merciful unto us and bless us : * and shew us the light of his countenance, and be merciful unto us.

That thy way may be known upon earth : * thy saving health among all nations.

Let the people praise thee, O God : * yea, let all the people praise thee.

O let the nations rejoice and be glad : * for thou shalt judge the folk righteously and govern the nations upon earth.

Let the people praise thee, O God : * let all the people praise thee.

Then shall the earth bring forth her increase :
* and God, even our own God, shall give us his
blessing.

God shall bless us : * and all the ends of the
world shall fear him.

Glory be.   As it was.

℣. Let us bless the Father and the Son with
the Holy Ghost.

℟. Let us praise and magnify him for ever.

℣. God hath given his Angels charge over
thee.

℟. To keep thee in all thy ways.

℣. O Lord, hear my prayer.

℟. And let my cry come unto thee.

℣. The Lord be with you.

℟. And with thy spirit.

Let us pray.   *Collect.*

VISIT, we beseech thee O Lord, this dwelling,
and drive far from it and from this thine handmaid N . . ., all the snares of the enemy : let thy
holy Angels dwell herein to preserve her and her
offspring in peace; and may thy bless ✠ ing be
upon her evermore.   Save them, almighty God,
and grant unto them thy perpetual light. Through
Christ, our Lord. ℟. Amen.

THE Blessing of God almighty, the Father, the
✠ Son, and the Holy Ghost, descend upon thee
and upon thine offspring, and remain with thee
alway. ℟. Amen.

BLESSING OF A WOMAN AFTER CHILDBIRTH

If a woman after childbirth, according to pious and laudable custom, desires to come to the Church to render thanks to God for her safety, and asks a blessing from the Priest, he shall come, vested in surplice and white stole, with a Clerk bearing the holy Water vessel, to the door of the Church, where he shall sprinkle her with holy Water, as she kneels at the threshold, holding a lighted candle; then shall he say:

℣. Our help is in the name of the Lord.

℟. Who hath made heaven and earth.

ANT. She shall receive.

PSALM 24. *Domini est terra.*

THE earth is the Lord's, and all that therein is: * the compass of the world, and they that dwell therein.

For he hath founded it upon the seas:* and prepared it upon the floods.

Who shall ascend into the hill of the Lord:* who shall rise up in his holy place?

Even he that hath clean hands and a pure heart:* and that hath not lift up his eyes unto vanity, nor sworn to deceive his neighbour.

He shall receive the blessing from the Lord:* and righteousness from the God of his salvation.

This is the generation of them that seek him:* even of them that seek thy face, O Jacob.

Lift up your heads, O ye gates, and be ye lift up, ye everlasting doors:* and the King of glory shall come in.

Who is the King of glory:* it is the Lord strong and mighty, even the Lord mighty in battle.

Lift up your heads, O ye gates, and be ye lift up, ye everlasting doors:* and the King of glory shall come in.

Who is the King of glory:* even the Lord of hosts, he is the King of glory.

Glory be.   As it was

ANT.   She shall receive the blessing from the Lord, and righteousness from the God of her salvation: for this is the generation of them that seek the Lord.

2.   Then placing in the hand of the woman the end of his stole, which hangs from his left shoulder, he leads her into the Church, saying:

Enter into the temple of God, adore the Son of the blessed Virgin Mary, who hath given thee fruitfulness of offspring.

3.   And she, having entered, kneels before the Altar and prays, giving thanks to God for the blessings bestowed upon her; then the Priest says:

> Kyrie, eléison.
> Christe, eléison.
> Kyrie, eléison.

Our Father, *secretly as far as:*

℣.   And lead us not into temptation.

℟.   But deliver us from evil.

℣. O Lord, save thy handmaid.

℟. My God, who trusteth in thee.

℣. O Lord, send her help from the sanctuary.

℟. And strengthen her out of Sion.

℣. Let the enemy have no advantage over her.

℟. Nor the son of wickedness approach to hurt her.

℣. O Lord, hear my prayer.

℟. And let my cry come unto thee.

℣. The Lord be with you.

℟. And with thy spirit.

Let us pray.   *Collect.*

ALMIGHTY and everlasting God, who through the childbearing of the blessed Virgin Mary hast turned the pains of the faithful who are with child into joy: look mercifully upon this thy handmaid, who cometh with gladness to thy holy temple to render thanks, and grant; that after this life, by the merits and intercession of the same blessed Mary, she may be worthy to attain with her child unto the joys of everlasting blessedness. Through Christ, our Lord. ℟. Amen.

4. *Then he sprinkles her again with holy Water, saying* :

The peace and blessing of God almighty, the Father, the Son, ✠ and the Holy Ghost, descend upon thee, and remain with thee alway. ℟. Amen.

THE CHURCHING OF WOMEN

(ACCORDING TO THE BOOK OF COMMON PRAYER.)

The woman at the usual time after her Delivery, shall come into the Church, decently apparelled, and there shall kneel down in some convenient place, as hath beeen accustomed, or as the Ordinary shall direct. And then the Priest shall say unto her:

FORASMUCH as it hath pleased almighty God of his goodness to give you a safe deliverance, and hath preserved you in the great danger of Child-birth; you shall therefore give hearty thanks unto God and say,

(Then shall the Priest say the 116th Psalm.)

PSALM 116. *Dilexi quoniam.*

I AM well pleased : that the Lord hath heard the voice of my prayer;

That he hath inclined his ear unto me : therefore will I call upon him as long as I live.

The snares of death compassed me round about : and the pains of hell gat hold upon me.

I found trouble and heaviness, and I called upon the name of the Lord : O Lord, I beseech thee, deliver my soul.

Gracious is the Lord and righteous : yea, our God is merciful.

The Lord preserveth the simple : I was in misery and he helped me.

Turn again then unto thy rest, O my soul : for the Lord hath rewarded thee.

And why? thou hast delivered my soul from death : and mine eyes from tears, and my feet from falling.

I will walk before the Lord : in the land of the living.

I believed, and therefore will I speak; but I was sore troubled : I said in my haste all men are liars.

What reward shall I give unto the Lord : for all the benefits that he hath done unto me?

I will receive the cup of salvation : and call upon the name of the Lord.

I will pay my vows now in the presence of all his people : in the courts of the Lord's house, even in the midst of thee, O Jerusalem.   Praise the Lord.

Glory be.   As it was.

Or, PSALM 127.   *Nisi Dominum.*

EXCEPT the Lord build the house : their labour is but lost that build it.

Except the Lord keep the city : the watchman waketh but in vain.

It is but lost labour that ye haste to rise up early, and so late take rest, and eat the bread of carefulness : for so he giveth his beloved sleep.

Lo, children and the fruit of the womb : are an heritage and gift that cometh of the Lord.

Like as the arrows in the hand of the giant : even so are the young children.

Happy is the man that hath his quiver full of them : they shall not be ashamed when they speak with their enemies in the gate.

Glory be.   As it was.

Then the Priest shall say:

LORD have mercy upon us.

Christ have mercy upon us.

Lord have mercy upon us.

OUR Father, which art in heaven, Hallowed be thy name. Thy kingdom come. Thy will be done, in earth as it is in heaven. Give us this day our daily bread. And forgive us our trespasses, As we forgive them that trespass against us. And lead us not into temptation; But deliver us from evil: For thine is the kingdom, the power, and the glory, For ever and ever. Amen.

Minister. O Lord save this woman, thy servant;

Answer. Who putteth her trust in thee.

Minister. Be thou to her a strong tower;

Answer. From the face of her enemy.

Minister. Lord, hear our prayer;

Answer. And let our cry come unto thee.

Minister: Let us pray.

O ALMIGHTY God, we give thee humble thanks for that thou hast vouchsafed to deliver this woman thy servant from the great pain and peril of Child-birth; Grant, we beseech thee, most merciful Father, that she, through thy help, may both faithfully live, and walk according to thy will in this life present; and also may be partaker of everlasting glory in the life to come; throgh Jesus Christ our Lord. *Amen.*

The woman that cometh to give her Thanks must offer accustomed Offerings, and if there be a Communion, it is convenient that she receive the holy Communion.

PART II.

LIST OF BLESSINGS.

(R) 1. Of Sacerdotal Vestments.
(R) 2. Of Altar Linen.
(R) 3. Of Corporals.
(R) 4. Of Tabernacle or Ciborium.
    5. Of a Cross or Crucifix.
(R) 6. Of a Monstrance.
(R) 7. Of a Reliquary.
    8. Of an Image.
    9. Of a Banner.
  10. Of Rosaries.
  11. Of Rosaries of The Seven Sorrows.
(R) 12. Of Holy Oil Stocks.
  13. Of Candles.
  14. Of a Foundation Stone.
  15. Of a House.
  16. Of Houses on Holy Saturday.
  17. Of a Domestic Oratory.
  18. Of a School House.
  19. Of an Organ.
  20. Of Crops or Harvest.
  21. Of a Carriage or Motor Car.
  22. Of a Ship or Boat.
  23. Consecration of a Paten and Chalice.
  24. Of Anything.

ALPHABETICAL INDEX OF FORMS OF BLESSING.

1. *The reserved blessings marked (R) above may only be given lawfully by the following:*

    a. All Bishops.

    b. Ordinaries, not being Bishops, for Churches in their own territory, e.g., Deans of Cathedrals and Peculiars.

    c. Parish Priests for Churches in their Parish, and Rectors of Churches for their Churches.

    d. Priests delegated by the Ordinary of the place.

6. Religious Superiors and Priests delegated by them for their own Churches and for Churches of nuns subject to them.

2. *Other blessings not marked (R) may be given by any Priest.*

3. *In all blessings outside Mass the Priest must wear at least a surplice and a stole of the colour of the Season, unless otherwise noted.*

4. *He must always bless standing and with head uncovered.*

At the beginning of each blessing, unless otherwise noted, he shall say:

℣. **Our help is in the name of the Lord.**

℟. **Who hath made heaven and earth.**

℣. **The Lord be with you.**

℟. **And with thy spirit.**

Then he shall say the appropriate Prayer or Prayers.

Afterwards he shall sprinkle with blessed Water, and if so noted, cense the object, saying nothing.

5. *When the Priest is to bless anything, he shall have a server with a vessel of blessed Water, and this book of the Ritual.*

6. *He shall take care not to place anything unseemly, such as eatables, on the Altar for blessing; but anything of that kind should be placed on a table, made ready in a suitable place.*

(1) BLESSING OF SACERDOTAL VESTMENTS IN GENERAL.

℣. **Our help.**

℣. **The Lord be with you.**

Let us pray. *Collect.*

A LMIGHTY and everlasting God, who by thy servant Moses didst decree that high-priestly and priestly and levitical vestments should be made for the fulfilment of their ministry in thy presence, to the honour and glory of thy name : graciously assist our supplications : that thou wouldest vouchsafe to pour out the showers of thy grace, and by thy mighty benediction through our lowly service to puri ✠ fy, bl ✠ ess, and conse ✠ crate these priestly vestments : that they may be rendered fit for thy divine service and thy holy mysteries, and blessed : and also may thy Bishops, Priests and Levites, clothed in these holy garments, be counted worthy to be strengthened and defended against all assaults or temptations of malignant spirits : and make them worthily and meetly to serve and cleave unto thy mysteries, and therein to persevere devoutly and acceptably unto thee. Through Christ, our Lord. ℞. Amen.

Let us pray. *Collect.*

O GOD, the creator and sanctifier of all things, who dost triumph in might invincible : graciously give heed to our prayers, and vouchsafe with thine own mouth to bl ✠ ess, sancti ✠ fy, and conse ✠ crate these garments òf the levitical, priestly and pontifical dignity, for the use of thy ministers : and vouchsafe to render all who use them meet for thy mysteries, that they doing thee devout and laudable service may be found accept-

able unto thee.   Through Christ, our Lord.
℟. Amen.

Let us pray.   *Collect.*

O LORD God almighty, who didst bid thy
servant Moses make for the High-priests,
Priests and Levites vestments needful for the service of the tabernacle of the covenant, and didst
replenish him with the spirit of wisdom for the
accomplishment of the same : vouchsafe to
bl ✠ ess, sancti ✠ fy, and conse ✠ crate these vestments for the service and worship of thy mysteries :
and vouchsafe that the ministers of thine altar who
shall be clothed in them may be meetly filled with
the grace of thy sevenfold Spirit, with the garment
of chastity and with the fruit of good works in
their ministry, which may win for them the bliss
of everlasting life.   Through Christ, our Lord.
℟. Amen.

And let them be sprinkled with holy Water.

(2)   BLESSING OF ALTAR CLOTHS OR ALTAR LINEN.

℣.   Our help.

℣.   The Lord be with you.

Let us pray.   *Collect.*

O LORD, graciously hear our prayers, and
vouchsafe to bl ✠ ess and sancti ✠ fy this
linen prepared for the service of thy holy Altar.
Through Christ, our Lord.   ℟. Amen.

Let us pray.   *Collect.*

O LORD, God almighty, who for forty days didst
teach thy servant Moses to make ornaments
and linen : the which also Miriam wove and made
for the service of the tabernacle of the covenant :
vouchsafe to bl ✠ ess, sancti ✠ fy and conse ✠ crate
these linen cloths for the covering and enveloping
of the Altar of thy most gracious Son, our Lord
Jesus Christ : Who with thee liveth and reigneth
in the unity of the Holy Spirit, God : world without end. ℟. Amen.

And let them be sprinkled with holy Water.

(3) BLESSING OF CORPORALS.

℣. Our help.

℣. The Lord be with you.

Let us pray.   *Collect.*

MOST gracious Lord, whose power is unspeakable, and whose mysteries are celebrated with
hidden wonders : grant we beseech thee, that this
linen cloth may be sancti ✠ fied by thy merciful
bene ✠ diction, that thereon may be consecrated
the Body and Blood of our Lord and God Jesus
Christ, thy Son : Who with thee liveth and
reigneth in the unity of the Holy Spirit, God :
world without end. ℟. Amen.

Let us pray.   *Collect.*

ALMIGHTY and everlasting God, vouchsafe to
bl ✠ ess, sancti ✠ fy and conse ✠ crate this
linen cloth, that it may cover and envelop the Body

N

and Blood of thy Son our Lord Jesus Christ : Who
with thee liveth and reigneth in the unity of the
Holy Spirit, God : world without end. ℞. Amen.

Let us pray. *Collect.*

ALMIGHTY God, shed upon our hands the help
of thy blessing : that through our bene ✠
diction this linen cloth may be sanctified, and may
be made by the grace of thy Holy Spirit a new
winding-sheet for the Body and Blood of our
Redeemer. Through the same Jesus Christ thy
Son our Lord : Who liveth and reigneth with thee
in the unity of the same Holy Spirit, . . . world
without end. ℞. Amen.

And let them be sprinkled with holy Water.

(4) BLESSING OF A TABERNACLE OR VESSEL FOR
    RESERVING THE MOST HOLY EUCHARIST.

℣. Our help is in the name of the Lord.
℞. Who hath made heaven and earth.
℣. The Lord be with you.
℞. And with thy spirit.

Let us pray. *Collect.*

ALMIGHTY and everlasting God, we humbly
beseech thy majesty : that thou wouldest
vouchsafe to hallow with the grace of thy bene ✠
diction this tabernacle (*or* vessel) fashioned to
contain the Body of thy Son our Lord Jesus Christ.
Through the same. ℞. Amen.

And let it be sprinkled with holy Water.

(5) THE BLESSING OF A CROSS OR CRUCIFIX.

If the Crosses are solemnly blessed and exposed for the veneration of the faithful, this blessing is reserved to the Ordinary, who may, however, delegate the hallowing to another priest. But if the blessing is used privately, any priest may perform it.

℣. Our help.
℣. The Lord be with you.

Let us pray.   *Collect.*

WE beseech thee, O Lord holy, Father almighty, everlasting God : that thou wouldest vouchsafe to ble ✠ ss this sign of the Cross that it may be a saving remedy for mankind; that it may stablish thy servants in faith, incite them to good works, and redeem their souls : and that it may be a solace, protection and defence against the fiery darts of their enemies. Through Christ, our Lord. ℟. Amen.

Let us pray.   *Collect.*

BLESS, O Lord Jesu Christ, this Cross, whereby thou didst deliver the world from the power of devils, and didst by thy Passion overcome the tempter to sin, who rejoiced in the transgression of the first man through taking of the forbidden tree. *(Here it is sprinkled with holy Water).* Be this sign of the Cross sanctified in the name of the Fa ✠ ther, and of the S ✠ on, and of the Holy ✠ Ghost : and may all, who for the Lord's sake pray and bow themselves before this Cross, find health of body and soul.   Through the same Christ, our Lord.   ℟. Amen.

Then shall the Priest and people, devoutly kneeling, venerate and kiss the Cross.

(6)   (R) THE BLESSING OF A MONSTRANCE FOR EXPOSING THE MOST HOLY SACRAMENT TO THE VENERATION OF THE FAITHFUL.

℣.   Our help.

℣.   The Lord be with you.

Let us pray.   *Collect.*

ALMIGHTY and everlasting God, vouchsafe to ble ✠ ss and sanc ✠ tify this vessel made for the exposing to the veneration of the faithful of the Body of thy Son, our Lord Jesus Christ : that all, who worship the same thine only-begotten Son in this world with godly affection, may in the world to come receive the everlasting reward of their piety.   Through the same Christ, our Lord. ℟. Amen.

And let it be sprinkled with holy Water.

(7)   (R) THE BLESSING OF A RELIQUARY.

℣.   Our help.

℣.   The Lord be with you.

Let us pray.   *Collect.*

BLE ✠ SS, O Lord, this vessel made ready to contain the Relics of thy Saints : and grant ; that whosoever shall venerate them with the affection

of their hearts may, at the intercession of the same
thy Saints, obtain pardon of all their sins and ever
be defended against all adversities. Through
Christ, our Lord. ℞. Amen.

And let it be sprinkled with holy Water.

(8) THE SOLEMN BLESSING OF AN IMAGE OF OUR LORD JESUS CHRIST OR THE B.V. MARY OR SOME OTHER SAINT.

If the images, being exposed to public venera-
tion, are solemnly blessed, this blessing is reserved to
the Ordinary, who may however delegate it to any
Priest. But this blessing may be performed privately
by any Priest without leave from the Ordinary.

℣. Our help.

℣. The Lord be with you.

Let us pray. *Collect.*

ALMIGHTY and everlasting God, who dost not
forbid the painting or carving of the images (*or*
likenesses) of thy Saints : to the end that as oft as
we look upon them with the eyes of the body, so
often, contemplating with the eyes of memory
their deeds and sanctity, we may imitate the same :
vouchsafe, we beseech thee, to ble ✠ ss and
sancti ✠ fy this picture (*or* image), fashioned to
the honour and memory of thine only-begotten
Son our Lord Jesus Christ (*or* the most blessed
Virgin Mary, Mother of our Lord Jesus Christ, *or*
blessed *N.* thine Apostle, *or* Martyr, *or* Bishop, *or*
Confessor, *or* blessed *N.* thy Virgin, *or* Martyr) :

and grant ; that whosoever before it shall study humbly to venerate and honour thine only-begotten Son (*or* the most blessed Virgin, *or* the glorious Apostles, *or* Martyr, *or* Bishop, *or* Confessor, *or* the glorious Virgin, *or* Martyr) may by *his* merits and intercession obtain in this world grace from thee, and in the world to come glory everlasting.   Through (the same) Christ, our Lord.   ℞. Amen.

And let it be sprinkled with holy Water.

(9) THE BLESSING OF A BANNER OF ANY SOCIETY.

℣.   Our help.

℣.   The Lord be with you.

Let us pray.   *Collect.*

O LORD Jesus Christ, whose Church is as an army set in array with banners : ble ✠ ss this banner ; that all who fight beneath it for thee, the Lord God of hosts, may, by the intercession of blessed *N . . .*, be made worthy to conquer their enemies, both visible and invisible, in this world, and after victory to triumph in the heavens. Through thee, Jesu Christ : Who with the Father and the Holy Ghost, livest and reignest God, world without end.   ℞. Amen.

And let it be sprinkled with holy Water.

(10)   THE BLESSING OF ROSARIES.

TO the praise and glory of the Virgin Mary, Mother of God, in memory of the mysteries of the life, death and resurrection of the same our

Lord Jesus Christ, may this chaplet of the most sacred Rosary be bless ✠ ed, and sanc ✠ tified : in the name of the Father, and of the Son, ✠ and of the Holy Ghost. Amen.

(11) The Blessing of Rosaries of the Seven Sorrows of Our Lady.

TO the praise and glory of the Virgin Mary, Mother of God, in memory of the Sorrows which she endured in the life and death of the same her Son, our Lord Jesus Christ, may this chaplet be bless ✠ ed and sanc ✠ tified : in the name of the Father, and of the Son, ✠ and of the Holy Ghost. Amen.

(12) (R) The Blessing of Stocks to contain the Holy Oils.

℣. Our help.

℣. The Lord be with you.

Let us pray. *Collect.*

HEARKEN unto our prayers, O Lord, most merciful Father : and vouchsafe to ble ✠ ss and sanc ✠ tify these vessels now to be purified, made ready for use in the sacred ministry of thy Church. Through Christ, our Lord. ℟. Amen.

Let us pray. *Collect.*

ALMIGHTY and everlasting God, by whom all unclean things are purified, and in whom all things which have been purified are enlightened : we humbly call upon thine almighty power, that every unclean spirit may be confounded and depart far from these vessels which thy servants offer unto thee ; that by thy bene ✠ diction they may abide holy for the use and ministry of thy Church. Through Christ, our Lord. ℞. Amen.

And let them be sprinkled with holy Water.

(13) THE BLESSING OF CANDLES.

All candles used in the church should be blessed before use.

℣. Our help.

℣. The Lord be with you.

Let us pray.   *Collect.*

O LORD Jesu Christ, Son of the living God, ble ✠ ss these candles at our supplication: pour upon them, O Lord, through the virtue of the holy Cro ✠ ss, thy heavenly benediction, who hast given them to drive away darkness from mankind : and let them receive such blessing by the sign of the holy Cro ✠ ss, that in whatsoever places they be kindled or set, the princes of darkness with all their ministers may depart, tremble and flee in terror from those habitations ; neither presume any more to disquiet or molest those who serve thee, the almighty God : Who livest and reignest, world without end. ℞. Amen.

And let them be sprinkled with holy Water.

(14) THE BLESSING OF A FOUNDATION STONE.

℣. Our help.

℣. The Lord be with you.

Let us pray. *Collect.*

O GOD, from whom every good work takes its beginning, and going forward ever receiveth an increase of perfection : grant our petitions, we beseech thee ; that the undertaking which we begin to the praise of thy name may, by the everlasting bounty of thy fatherly wisdom, be brought to fulfilment. Through Christ, our Lord. ℞. Amen.

And let it be sprinkled with holy Water.

(15) THE BLESSING OF A HOUSE.

℣. Our help.

℣. The Lord be with you.

Let us pray. *Collect.*

WE humbly beseech thee, O God the Father almighty, on behalf of this house, of them that dwell herein, and of all things belonging to them ; that it may please thee to ble ✠ ss and sancti ✠ fy it and to replenish it with all good things ; grant unto them, O Lord, abundance of the dew of heaven, and of the fatness of the earth for their sustenance, and so direct the desires of their hearts that they may effectually obtain thy mercy. At our coming in, therefore, vouchsafe to ble ✠ ss and sancti ✠ fy this house, even as thou didst vouchsafe to bless the house of Abraham, Isaac, and Jacob : and grant that within the walls of this house the Angels of thy light may dwell, and guard it and them that dwell therein. Through Christ, our Lord. ℞. Amen.

And let it be sprinkled with holy Water.

(16) Blessing of Houses
on Holy Saturday and throughout Eastertide.

The Parish Priest, or another Priest by his leave, vested in surplice and white stole, with a server bearing a vessel of Water blessed in the baptismal Font, and taken therefrom before the inpouring of oil and Chrism, on Holy Saturday visits the houses of his parish, sprinkling them with the same blessed Water.

On entering a house he says:

℣. Peace be to this house.

℟. And to all that dwell in it.

Then sprinkling the principal rooms and those who live in the house, he says the Antiphon:

I beheld water issuing out from the temple, alleluia: and all to whom that water came were saved, and they shall say, alleluia, alleluia.

Psalm 118. O give thanks unto the Lord, for he is gracious: because his mercy endureth for ever.

℣. Glory be.

Ant. I beheld, etc.

℣. O Lord, shew thy mercy upon us, alleluia.

℟. And grant us thy salvation, alleluia.

℣. O Lord, hear my prayer.

℟. And let my cry come unto thee.

℣. The Lord be with you.

℟. And with thy spirit.

Let us pray. *Collect.*

GRACIOUSLY hear us, O Lord holy, Father almighty, everlasting God : and as thou didst guard from the destroying Angel the houses of the Hebrews, when they went out of Egypt, being sprinkled with the blood of the lamb, (which prefigured our Passover wherein Christ is sacrificed); so vouchsafe to send thy holy Angel from heaven to guard, cherish, protect, visit and defend all who dwell in this dwelling-place. Through the same Christ, our Lord. ℟. Amen.

Then the Priest sprinkles the other rooms in order, saying nothing.

(17) THE BLESSING OF A DOMESTIC ORATORY.

℣. Our help.

℣. The Lord be with you.

Let us pray. *Collect.*

O GOD, who dost hallow places which are to be dedicated to thy name : pour thy grace upon this house of prayer : that all who herein call upon thy name may know the succour of thy mercy. ℟. Amen.

And let it be sprinkled with holy Water.

(18) THE BLESSING OF A SCHOOL HOUSE.

The Priest on entering shall sprinkle the rooms with holy Water, saying:

℣. Peace be to this house.

℟. And to all that dwell in it.

℣. Our help is in the name of the Lord.
℞. Who hath made heaven and earth.
℣. The Lord be with you.
℞. And with thy spirit.

Let us pray. *Collect.*

O LORD Jesu Christ, who didst command thine Apostles, that into whatsoever house they entered they should pray for peace upon it; sancti ✠ fy, we beseech thee, by our ministry this house destined for the education of boys (*or* girls); pour thy bene ✠ diction upon it, and abundance of peace ; let salvation come to it, even as it came to the house of Zacchæus, at thy entering ; command thine Angels to keep it and to drive far from it all the power of the enemy ; fill with the spirit of knowledge, wisdom and thy fear them that teach therein ; nourish with thy heavenly grace them that learn ; and grant that they may understand those things which for their salvation they are taught, may keep them in their hearts and practise them in their works ; and may all that dwell therein please thee by works of every virtue, that they may be worthy to be received hereafter to their everlasting home in heaven. Through thee, O Jesu Christ, Saviour of the world, who livest and reignest God, world without end. ℞. Amen.

(19) The Blessing of an Organ in the Church.

℣. Our help is in the name of the Lord.
℞. Who hath made heaven and earth.

Psalm 150. *Laudate Dominum.*

O PRAISE God in his holiness : * praise him in the firmament of his power.

Praise him in his noble acts : * praise him according to his excellent greatness.

Praise him in the sound of the trumpet : * praise him upon the lute and harp.

Praise him in the cymbals and dances : * praise him upon the strings and pipe.

Praise him upon the well-tuned cymbals : * praise him upon the loud cymbals.

Let everything that hath breath : * praise the Lord.

Glory be. As it was.

℣. Praise the Lord in the cymbals and dances.

℟. Praise him upon the strings and pipe.

℣. The Lord be with you.

℟. And with thy spirit.

Let us pray.   *Collect.*

O GOD, who through thy servant Moses didst command that trumpets should be made to sound over the sacrifices to be offered to thy name ; and who through the children of Israel didst will that the praise of thy name should be proclaimed in the trumpets and cymbals : ble ✠ ss, we beseech thee, this instrument of the organ now dedicated to thy worship ; and grant that thy faithful, who praise thee on earth with spiritual songs, may be made worthy to attain unto everlasting joys in

heaven. Through Jesus Christ thy Son, our Lord :
Who liveth. ℟. Amen.

And let it be sprinkled with holy Water.

(20) THE BLESSING OF CROPS OR HARVEST.

℣. Our help.

℣. The Lord be with you.

Let us pray. *Collect.*

O LORD GOD almighty, who ceasest not to
bestow on men abundance of the dew of
heaven and the substance of the fatness of the
earth : we render thanks to thy most gracious
majesty for the fruits that have been gathered,
beseeching thy mercy ; that thou wouldest vouchsafe to ble ✠ ss, preserve and defend from all harm
these crops, which of thy goodness we have
received : and grant therewith ; that they, whose
desire thou hast fulfilled with good things, may
glory in thy protection, may continually praise thy
mercies, and may so pass through good things
temporal, that they lose not the things eternal.
Through Christ, our Lord. ℟. Amen.

And let them be sprinkled with holy Water.

(21) THE BLESSING OF A CARRIAGE OR MOTOR CAR.

℣. Our help.

℟. The Lord be with you.

Let us pray. *Collect.*

A SSIST us mercifully, O Lord, in these our
supplications, and ble ✠ ss this carriage with
thy holy right hand : join unto it thy holy Angels,
that they may alway deliver and defend all who
ride therein from every peril ; and as thou didst
give faith and grace by thy Levite Philip unto the
man of Ethiopia as he sat upon his chariot and read
thy sacred words; so unto thy servants shew the
way of salvation, that they who by the help of thy
grace are ever intent upon good works, may, after
all the changes and chances of the journey of this
life, be worthy to obtain eternal joys. Through
Christ, our Lord. ℟. Amen.

And let it be sprinkled with holy Water.

(22) THE BLESSING OF A SHIP OR BOAT.

℣. Our help.

℟. The Lord be with you.

Let us pray. *Collect.*

B E favourable, O Lord, unto our supplications,
and with thy holy right hand ble ✠ ss this
ship and all them that shall journey therein ; even
as thou didst vouchsafe to bless the ark of Noe ;
stretch forth unto them, O Lord, thy right hand,
as thou didst stretch it forth unto blessed Peter
when he walked upon the sea ; and send thy holy
Angel from heaven to keep and deliver it always
from every peril, together with all that shall be
therein : and, all adversities being driven away,
preserve thy servants in the haven where they

would be, giving them peaceful voyaging : and, their business ended and rightly fulfilled, vouchsafe in due time to bring them again with all gladness to their homes : Who livest and reignest world without end. ℞. Amen.

And let it be sprinkled with holy Water.

(23) ORDER FOR THE CONSECRATION OF A PATEN AND CHALICE.

A Bishop, wishing to proceed to the consecration of a Chalice, or any vestment or ecclesiastical ornament, should always have a stole about his neck, and may wear a mitre, when it is fitting.

This Blessing may be done in any place or at any time that the Bishop may appoint.

In the consecration of a Paten, for which the holy Chrism must be made ready, and a vessel of holy water with the sprinkler, the Bishop, standing and wearing the mitre, says :

℣. Our help is in the name of the Lord.

℞. Who hath made heaven and earth.

LET us pray, dearly beloved brethren, that the blessing of divine grace may consecrate and sanctify this Paten (these Patens), for the breaking thereon of the Body of our Lord Jesus Christ, who endured the suffering of the Cross for the salvation of us all.

Then, laying aside the mitre, he says :

℣. The Lord be with you.

℞. And with thy spirit.

Let us pray.

ALMIGHTY and everlasting God, who didst institute the sacrifices of the law, and who didst command the finest wheat flour, scattered among them, to be borne to thy altar on patens of gold and silver : vouchsafe to ble ✠ ss, sancti ✠ fy and conse ✠ crate this Paten (these Patens) for the ministration of the Eucharist of Jesus Christ thy Son, who for our salvation and for that of all willed himself to be sacrificed unto thee, O God the Father, on the gibbet of the Cross, and liveth and reigneth with thee in the unity of the Holy Ghost . . . ℟. Amen.

Then the Bishop, receiving the mitre, dipping the thumb of his right hand in the Chrism, makes therewith a Cross over the Paten (each Paten) from rim to rim, and then anoints all the surface with his thumb, saying :

VOUCHSAFE, O Lord God, to conse ✠ crate and sancti ✠ fy this Paten through this anointing, and our bene ✠ diction in Christ Jesu our Lord : Who liveth and reigneth with thee in the unity of the Holy Ghost . . . ℟. Amen.

Then, still standing with the mitre, he proceeds to the blessing of the Chalice, saying :

LET us pray, dearly beloved brethren, that our God and Lord may sanctify by the inspiration of his heavenly grace this Chalice (these Chalices) to be consecrated to the use of his service : and that he may join the fulness of divine favour to this consecration by man.   Through Christ, our Lord.   ℟. Amen.

Then, laying aside the mitre, he says :

℣. The Lord be with you.

℟. And with thy spirit.

Let us pray.

VOUCHSAFE, O Lord our God, to ble ✠ ss this Chalice (these Chalices), fashioned by the godly devotion of thy servants to the use of thy ministry, and to fill it (them) with that sancti ✠ fication, wherewith thou didst fill the hallowed chalice of Melchisedech thy servant : and let that, which by art or the nature of metal cannot be worthy of thine altars, be sanctified by thy bene ✠ diction. Through. ℟. Amen.

Then, receiving the mitre, he makes a cross with the thumb of his right hand from the Chrism within the Chalice itself (each Chalice) from lip to lip, and then anoints the whole of the interior, saying :

VOUCHSAFE, O Lord God, to conse ✠ crate and sancti ✠ fy this Chalice through this anointing, and our bene ✠ diction in Christ Jesu our Lord : Who liveth and reigneth with thee, in the unity of the Holy Ghost . . . ℟. Amen.

Then, laying aside the mitre, he says over the Chalices and Patens :

℣. The Lord be with you.

℟. And with thy spirit.

Let us pray.

ALMIGHTY and everlasting God, pour forth, we beseech thee, the power of thy benediction on our hands : that through our bene ✠ diction this Vessel and Paten (these Vessels and Patens) may be sanctified, and be made by the grace of the Holy Ghost a new sepulchre for the Body and Blood of our Lord Jesus Christ. Through the same . . . in the unity of the same Holy Ghost . . . ℞. Amen.

Lastly he sprinkles the Chalice and Paten (Chalices and Patens) with holy Water, which should be done after all blessings of any kind. Which done, he causes the Patens and Chalices to be wiped by some Priest with bread crumbs, and well cleansed; then the wipings are thrown into the fire or the sacrarium.

(24) THE BLESSING OF ANYTHING FOR WHICH A SPECIAL FORM IS NOT PROVIDED.

℣.   Our help.

℣.   The Lord be with you.

Let us pray.   *Collect.*

O GOD, by whose word all things are sanctified : pour thy bene ✠ diction upon this creature (these creatures) ; and grant that whosoever shall use it (them) with thanksgiving according to thy law and will, may, by the invocation of thy most holy name, receive from thee, who art its (their) maker, health of body and protection of soul. Through Christ, our Lord. ℞. Amen.

And let it (or them) be sprinkled with holy Water.

ORDO

AD FACIENDAM AQUAM BENEDICTAM.

(For English version, see page 215.)

Diebus Dominicis, et quandocumque opus sit, præparato sale et aqua munda benedicenda in ecclesia, vel in sacristia, Sacerdos, superpelliceo et stola violacea indutus, primo dicit :

℣. Adjutórium nostrum in nómine Dómini.

℟. Qui fecit cælum et terram.

2. Deinde absolute incipit exorcismum salis :

EXORCIZO te, creatúra salis, per Deum ✠ vivum, per Deum ✠ verum, per Deum ✠ sanctum, per Deum, qui te per Eliséum Prophétam in aquam mitti jussit, ut sanarétur sterílitas aquæ : ut efficiáris sal exorcizátum in salútem credéntium ; et sis ómnibus suméntibus te sánitas ánimæ et córporis ; et effúgiat, atque discédat a loco, in quo aspérsum fúeris, omnis phantásia, et nequítia, vel versútia diabólicæ fraudis, omnísque spíritus immúndus, adjurátus per eum, qui ventúrus est judicáre vivos et mórtuos, et sæculum per ignem. ℟. Amen.

Orémus.   *Oratio.*

IMMENSAM cleméntiam tuam, omnípotens ætérne Deus, humíliter implorámus, ut hanc creatúram salis, quam in usum géneris humáni tribuísti, bene ✠ dícere et sancti ✠ ficáre tua pietáte dignéris : ut sit ómnibus suméntibus salus mentis et córporis ; et quidquid ex eo tactum vel respérsum fúerit, cáreat omni immundítia, omníque impugnatióne spirituális nequítiæ. Per Dóminum nostrum. ℟. Amen.

Exorcismus aquæ : et dicitur absolute :

EXORCIZO te, creatúra aquæ, in nómine Dei Patris ✠ omnipoténtis, et in nómine Jesu ✠ Christi, Fílii ejus, Dómini nostri, et in virtúte Spíritus ✠ Sancti : ut fias aqua exorcizáta ad effugándam omnem potestátem inimíci, et ipsum inimícum eradicáre et explantáre váleas cum ángelis suis apostáticis, per virtútem ejúsdem Dómini nostri Jesu Christi : qui ventúrus est judicáre vivos et mórtuos, et sæculum per ignem. ℟. Amen.

Orémus.   *Oratio.*

DEUS, qui ad salútem humáni géneris máxima quæque sacraménta in aquárum substántia condidísti : adésto propítius invocatiónibus nostris, et eleménto huic multímodis purificatiónibus præparáto, virtútem tuæ bene ✠ dictiónis infúnde : ut creatúra tua, mystériis tuis sérviens, ad abigéndos dæmones, morbósque pelléndos, divinæ grátiæ sumat efféctum ; ut quidquid in dómibus, vel in locis fidélium, hæc unda respérserit, cáreat omni immundítia, liberétur a noxa : non illic resídeat spíritus péstilens, non aura corrúmpens : discédant omnes insídiæ laténtis inimíci; et si quid est, quod aut incolumitáti habitántium ínvidet, aut quiéti, aspersióne hujus aquæ effúgiat : ut salúbritas per invocatiónem sancti tui nóminis expetíta, ab ómnibus sit impugnatiónibus defénsa. Per Dóminum nostrum. ℟. Amen.

3. *Hic ter mittat sal in aquam in modum crucis, dicendo semel :*

Commíxtio salis et aquæ páriter fiat, in nómine Pa ✠ tris, et Fí ✠ lii, et Spíritus ✠ Sancti.

℞. Amen.

℣. Dóminus vobíscum. ℞. Et cum spíritu tuo.

Orémus. *Oratio.*

DEUS, invíctæ virtútis auctor, et insuperábilis imperii Rex, ac semper magníficus triumphátor : qui advérsæ dominatiónis vires réprimis : qui inimíci rugiéntis sævítiam súperas : qui hostíles nequítias poténter expúgnas : te, Dómine, treméntes et súpplices deprecámur, ac pétimus : ut hanc creatúram salis et aquæ dignánter aspícias, benígnus illústres, pietátis tuæ rore sanctíficres ; ut, ubicúmque fúerit aspérsa, per invocatiónem sancti nóminis tui, omnis infestátio immúndi spíritus abigátur, terrórque venenósi serpéntis procul pellátur : et præséntia Sancti Spíritus nobis, misericórdiam tuam poscéntibus, ubíque adésse dignétur. Per Dóminum nostrum Jesum Christum Fílium tuum : Qui tecum vivit et regnat in unitáte ejúsdem Spíritus Sancti Deus, per ómnia sæcula sæculórum. ℞. Amen.

4. *Post benedictionem aquæ, Sacerdos Dominicis diebus, antequam incipiat Missam, aspergit Altare, deinde se, et Ministros, ac populum, prout in Missali praescribitur, et in Appendice huius Ritualis (p. 249) habetur.*

THE ORDER FOR BLESSING OF WATER.

(For Latin version, see page 212.)

On Sundays and. whenever necessary, salt and the water to be blessed being made ready in the Sacristy, the Priest, vested in surplice with violet stole, first says:

℣. Our help is in the name of the Lord.

℞. Who hath made heaven and earth.

2. *Then he straightway begins the exorcism of the salt.*

I ADJURE thee, O creature of salt, by the living ✠ God, by the true ✠ God, by the holy ✠ God: by God who commanded thee to be cast by the prophet Eliseus into the water to heal the barrenness thereof: that thou become salt exorcised for the health of them that believe: be thou to all them that take of thee for healing of soul and body: let all vain·imaginations, wickedness, and subtlety of the wiles of the devil, let every unclean spirit flee and depart from the place where thou shalt be sprinkled, adjured by him who shall come to judge the quick and the dead, and the world by fire. ℞. Amen.

Let us pray. *Collect.*

ALMIGHTY and everlasting God, we humbly beseech thine infinite mercy: that thou wouldest vouchsafe of thy loving-kindness to ble✠ss and sancti✠fy this creature of salt, which thou hast given for the use of mankind; that it may be unto all that take of it health of mind and body; and let all such things as shall be touched or sprinkled there-

with be free from all uncleanness, and from all
assaults of spiritual wickedness. Through. ℟.
Amen.

Exorcism of the water: and straightway is said:

I ADJURE thee, O creature of water, in the name
of God ✠ the Father almighty, in the name of
Jesus ✠ Christ his Son, our Lord, and by the power
of the Holy ✠ Ghost: that thou become water
exorcised for the putting to flight of all the power
of the enemy, and that thou be enabled to root out
and expel the enemy himself with his apostate
angels by the power of the same Jesus Christ our
Lord: who shall come to judge the quick and the
dead, and the world by fire. ℟. Amen.

Let us pray. *Collect.*

O GOD, who for the salvation of mankind hast
ordained in thy chiefest sacraments the use of
the substance of water: mercifully assist us who
call upon thee, and pour the power of thy bene-
✠diction upon this element, made ready by divers
cleansings: that this thy creature, in the service of
thy mysteries, may effectually receive thy divine
grace for the casting forth of devils and the healing
of diseases, that whatsoever in the dwellings or
abodes of thy faithful people shall be sprinkled
with this water may be free from all uncleanness
and delivered from all evil: let not the spirit of
pestilence abide therein, nor the breath of corruption; let all the snares of the unseen enemy depart
from thence: and let all such things as are contrary

to the health and peace of them that dwell therein
be put to flight by the sprinkling of this water;
that, as through the invocation of thy holy name
we entreat for them thy saving health, so they may
be defended against all assaults.   Through.   ℞.
Amen.

*3.   Here he thrice casts the salt into the water in the
form of a cross, saying once :*

LET this commingling of salt and water be
wrought in the Name of the Fa✠ther, and of
the So✠n, and of the Holy ✠ Ghost.   ℞.   Amen.

℣.   The Lord be with you.

℞.   And with thy spirit.

Let us pray.   *Collect.*

O GOD, who art the author of strength invincible, the King of the empire that none may
overcome, who art ever glorious in thy triumphs :
who dost quell the might of the dominion that is
against thee, who rulest the raging of the fierce
enemy, who dost overthrow by thy power the
wickedness of thy foes: we entreat thee, O Lord,
and beseech thee in fear and lowliness: that thou
wouldest graciously behold this creature of salt
and water, and mercifully enlighten and sanctify
it with the dew of thy loving-kindness; that,
wheresoever it shall be sprinkled, all the snares of
the unclean spirit may through the invocation of
thy holy name be driven away, and the dread of
the poisonous serpent be cast forth: and in all
places let the presence of the Holy Ghost be vouch-

safed unto us who call upon thy mercy. Through
. . . . . . in the unity of the same Holy Ghost.
℟. **Amen.**

4. *After the blessing of the water, the Priest on
Sundays, before he begins the Mass, sprinkles the
Altar, then himself, the Ministers and the people, as
is prescribed in the Missal, and given in the Appendix
of this Ritual (page 249).*

APPENDIX

BENEDICTIO SANCTISSIMI SACRAMENTI.

(For English version, see page 221).

O SALUTARIS Hóstia,
  Quae caeli pandis óstium,
Bella premunt hostília;
Da robur, fer auxílium.

Uni trinóque Dómino
Sit sempitérna glória :
Qui vitam sine término
Nobis donet in pátria. Amen.

Here may follow a Litany or other devotions.
Then is sung :

TANTUM ergo Sacraméntum
  Venerémur cérnui :
Et antíquum documéntum
Novo cedat rítui :
Præstet fides suppleméntum
Sénsuum deféctui.

Genitóri Genitóque
Laus et jubilátio,
Salus, honor, virtus quoque
Sit et benedíctio :
Procedénti ab utróque
Compar sit laudátio. Amen.

℣. Panem de caelo præstitísti eis.
℞. Omne delectaméntum in se habéntem.

Tempore paschali, et die festo et per totam
octavam Corporis Christi additur Alleluia.

Orémus. *Oratio.*

DEUS, qui nobis sub Saceaménto mirábili passionis tuæ memóriam reliquísti : tríbue, quaesumus, ita nos Córporis et Sánguinis tui sacra mystéria venerári ; ut redemptiónis tuae fructum in nobis júgiter sentiámus : Qui vivis et regnas in saecula saeculórum. ℞. Amen.

Then are usually said :

THE DIVINE PRAISES.

Blessed be God.

Blessed be his holy Name.

Blessed be Jesus Christ, true God and true Man.

Blessed be the Name of Jesus.

Blessed be his most sacred Heart.

Blessed be Jesus in the most holy Sacrament of the Altar.

Blessed be the great Mother of God, Mary most holy.

Blessed be her holy and immaculate Conception.

Blessed be the name of Mary, Virgin and Mother.

Blessed be Saint Joseph, her most chaste Spouse.

Blessed be God in his Angels and his Saints.

Then may be sung :

ANT. Adorémus in ætérnum sanctíssimum Saceaméntum.

PSALM 116.

LAUDATE Dóminum, omnes gentes : * laudáte eum, omnes populi.

Quóniam confirmáta est super nos miseri-córdia ejus: * et véritas Dómini manet in ætérnum.

Glória Patri, et Fílio : * et Spirítui Sancto.

Sicut erat in princípio, et nunc, et semper : * et in sæcula sæculórum. Amen.

ANT. Adorémus in æternum sanctíssimum Sacraméntum.

BENEDICTION OF THE MOST HOLY SACRAMENT.

(*For Latin version see page* 219.)

O SAVING Victim, opening wide
  The gate of heaven to man below :
Our foes press hard on every side ;
Thine aid supply, thy strength bestow.

All praise and thanks to thee ascend
For evermore, blest One in Three :
O grant us life that shall not end,
In our true native land with thee. Amen.

Here may follow a Litany or other devotions.

Then is sung :

THEREFORE we, before him bending,
  This great Sacrament revere ;
Types and shadows have their ending,
For the newer rite is here ;
Faith, our outward sense befriending,
Makes the inward vision clear.

Glory let us give, and blessing
To the Father and the Son ;
Honour, might and praise addressing,
While eternal ages run ;
Ever too his love confessing,
Who, from both, with both is one.   Amen.

℣.   Thou gavest them bread from heaven.
(Alleluia.)
℟.   Containing in itself all sweetness.

Alleluia *is added in Eastertide, and on the Feast and
through the Octave of Corpus Christi.*

Let us pray.   *Collect.*

O GOD, who under a wonderful Sacrament hast
left unto us a memorial of thy passion : grant
us, we beseech thee, so to venerate the sacred
mysteries of thy Body and Blood ; that we may
ever perceive within ourselves the fruit of thy
redemption : Who livest and reignest, world
without end.   ℟. Amen.

Then are usually said :

THE DIVINE PRAISES.

BLESSED be God.
Blessed be his holy Name.
Blessed be Jesus Christ, true God and true Man.
Blessed be the Name of Jesus.
Blessed be his most sacred Heart.
Blessed be Jesus in the most holy Sacrament of
the Altar.

Blessed be the great Mother of God, Mary most
    holy.
Blessed be her holy and immaculate Conception.
Blessed be the name of Mary, Virgin and Mother.
Blessed be Saint Joseph, her most chaste Spouse.
Blessed be God in his Angels and his Saints.

Then may be sung:

ANT. Let us adore for ever the Most Holy
Sacrament.

PSALM 117. *Laudate Dominum.*

O PRAISE the Lord, all ye heathen : * praise
    him, all ye nations.
    For his merciful kindness is ever more and
more towards us : * and the truth of the Lord
endureth for ever.
    Glory be to the Father, and to the Son : * and
to the Holy Ghost.
    As it was in the beginning, is now, and ever
shall be : * world without end. Amen.

ANT. Let us adore for ever the Most Holy
Sacrament.

LITANY OF THE MOST HOLY NAME OF JESUS.

KYRIE, eléison, *or* Lord, have mercy.
    Christe, eléison, *or* Christ, have mercy.
    Kyrie, eléison, *or* Lord, have mercy.
Jesu, hear us.
Jesu, graciously hear us.
O God the Father, of heaven, *Have mercy upon us.*
O God the Son, Redeemer of the world,

O God the Holy Ghost,
Holy Trinity, One God,
Jesu, Son of the living God,
Jesu, Splendour of the Father,
Jesu, Brightness of the eternal light,
Jesu, King of glory.
Jesu, Sun of righteousness,
Jesu, Son of the Virgin Mary,
Jesu, most lovable,
Jesu, most wonderful,
Jesu, mighty God,
Jesu, Father of the world to come,
Jesu, Angel of great counsel,
Jesu, most powerful,
Jesu, most patient,
Jesu, most obedient,
Jesu, meek and lowly of heart,
Jesu, lover of chastity,
Jesu, who lovest us,
Jesu, God of peace,
Jesu, Author of life,
Jesu, Pattern of virtues,
Jesu, zealous lover of souls,
Jesu, our God,
Jesu, our Refuge,
Jesu, Father of the poor,
Jesu, Treasure of the faithful,
Jesu, good Shepherd,
Jesu, true Light,
Jesu, eternal Wisdom,
Jesu, infinite Goodness,
Jesu, our way and our life,

Jesu, Joy of Angels,
Jesu, King of Patriarchs,
Jesu, Master of Apostles,
Jesu, Teacher of Evangelists,
Jesu, Strength of Martyrs,
Jesu, Light of Confessors,
Jesu, Purity of Virgins,
Jesu, Crown of all Saints.
Be thou merciful, *Spare us, Jesu.*
Be thou merciful, *Hear us, Jesu.*
From all evil, *Deliver us, Jesu.*
From all sin,
From thy wrath,
From the snares of the devil,
From the spirit of fornication,
From everlasting death,
From neglect of thy inspirations,
By the mystery of thy holy Incarnation,
By thy Nativity.
By thine Infancy,
By thy most divine Life,
By thy Labours,
By thine Agony and Passion,
By thy Cross and Dereliction,
By thy Weariness,
By thy Death and Burial,
By thy Resurrection,
By thine Ascension,
By thine Institution of the most holy Eucharist,
By thy Joys,
By thy Glory,

P

O Lamb of God, that takest away the sins of the
world,
 Spare us, Jesu.
O Lamb of God, that takest away the sins of the
world,
 Hear us, Jesu.
O Lamb of God, that takest away the sins of the
world,
 Have mercy upon us, Jesu.
Jesu, hear us.
Jesu, graciously hear us.

Let us pray.   *Collect.*

O LORD Jesu Christ, who hast said : Ask, and
ye shall receive; seek, and ye shall find;
knock, and it shall be opened unto you : We
beseech thee, grant unto us that ask the affection
of thy most divine love; that loving thee with our
whole heart, we may shew forth thy love in word
and deed, and may never cease from thy praise.

O LORD, who never failest to help and govern
them whom thou dost bring up in thy steadfast fear and love : Keep us, we beseech thee,
under the protection of thy good providence; and
make us to have a perpetual fear and love of thy
holy Name; Who livest and reignest, world
without end. ℞. Amen.

LITANY OF THE BLESSED VIRGIN MARY.

KYRIE, eléison, *or* Lord, have mercy.
Christe, eléison, *or* Christ, have mercy.
 Kyrie, eléison, *or* Lord, have mercy.

O Christ, hear us.
O Christ, graciously hear us.
O God the Father, of heaven, *Have mercy upon us.*
O God the Son, Redeemer of the world,
O God the Holy Ghost,
Holy Trinity, One God.
Holy Mary, *Pray for us.*
Holy Mother of God,
Holy Virgin of virgins,
Mother of Christ,
Mother of divine grace,
Mother most pure,
Mother most chaste,
Mother inviolate,
Mother undefiled,
Mother most lovable,
Mother most wonderful,
Mother of good Counsel,
Mother of the Creator,
Mother of the Saviour,
Virgin most prudent,
Virgin most worshipful,
Virgin most renowned,
Virgin most mighty,
Virgin most gentle,
Virgin most faithful,
Mirror of righteousness,
Seat of Wisdom,
Cause of our gladness,
Vessel of the Spirit,
Vessel of honour,
Vessel of devotion wondrous,

Mystic Rose,
Tower of David,
Tower of ivory,
House of gold,
Ark of the Covenant,
Gate of heaven,
Star of the Morning,
Salvation of the weak,
Refuge of sinners,
Consoler of the afflicted,
Help of Christians,
Queen of Angels,
Queen of Patriarchs,
Queen of Prophets,
Queen of Apostles,
Queen of Martyrs,
Queen of Confessors,
Queen of Virgins,
Queen of all Saints,
Queen conceived without original sin,
Queen of the most holy Rosary,
Queen of Peace,
O Lamb of God, that takest away the sins of the
    world,
    Spare us, O Lord.
O Lamb of God, that takest away the sins of the
    world,
    Hear us, O Lord.
O Lamb of God, that takest away the sins of the
    world,
    Have mercy upon us.

℣. Pray for us, O holy Mother of God :

℟. That we may be made worthy of the promises of Christ.

Let us pray. *Collect.*

G RANT, we beseech thee, O Lord God, that we thy servants may enjoy perpetual health of mind and of body : and at the glorious intercession of blessed Mary ever Virgin, be delivered from present sadness, and rejoice in everlasting gladness. Through Christ, our Lord. ℟. Amen.

FOR THANKSGIVING.

The Ambrosian Hymn is sung on occasions of special thanksgiving after Mass, or as a separate function, or during Benediction, as may be appointed. It is sung during Benediction on New Year's Eve, December 31st, and on the evening of the Sunday within the Octave of Corpus Christi, before the Tantum ergo.

At Benediction while the Priest intones We praise thee, O God, *he himself and all others kneel: then all stand, and the Choir continues: otherwise all stand from the beginning.*

Te Deum laudamus.

WE praise thee, O God : * we acknowledge thee to be the Lord.

All the earth doth worship thee : * the Father everlasting.

To thee all Angels cry aloud: * the Heavens and all the Powers therein.

To thee Cherubim and Seraphim : * continually do cry :

Holy,

Holy,

Holy, * Lord God of Sabaoth.

Heaven and earth are full: * of the majesty of thy glory.

The glorious company of the Apostles: * praise thee.

The goodly fellowship of the Prophets : * praise thee.

The noble army of Martyrs: * praise thee.

The holy Church throughout all the world: * doth acknowledge thee.

The Father: * of an infinite majesty.

Thine honourable, true: * and only Son;

Also the Holy Ghost : * the Comforter.

Thou art the everlasting Son: * of the Father.

When thou tookest upon thee to deliver man: * thou didst not abhor the Virgin's womb.

When thou hadst overcome the sharpness of death: * thou didst open the kingdom of heaven to all believers.

Thou sittest at the right hand of God: * in the glory of the Father.

We believe that thou shalt come: * to be our Judge.

The following verse is sung kneeling.

We therefore pray thee, help thy servants: * whom thou hast redeemed with thy precious blood.

Make them to be numbered with thy Saints: * in glory everlasting.

O Lord, save thy people: * and bless thine heritage.

Govern them: * and lift them up for ever.

Day by day: * we magnify thee;

And we worship thy name: * ever world without end.

Vouchsafe, O Lord: * to keep us this day without sin.

O Lord have mercy upon us: * have mercy upon us.

O Lord, let thy mercy lighten upon us: * as our trust is in thee.

O Lord, in thee have I trusted: * let me never be confounded.

(At Benediction all kneel, the Priest included: otherwise all stand till the end of the Collect.)

℣. Let us bless the Father and the Son with the Holy Spirit.†

℞. Let us praise him and magnify him above all for ever.

℣. Blessed art thou, O Lord, in the firmament of heaven.

℞. And worthy to be praised and glorious, and magnified above all for ever.

℣. O Lord, hear my prayer.

℞. And let my cry come unto thee.

[At Benediction the Priest alone now stands.]

℣. The Lord be with you.

℞. And with thy spirit.

Let us pray.   *Collect.*

O GOD, whose mercies are without number, and the treasure of whose goodness is infinite: we render thanks to thy most gracious majesty for the gifts thou hast bestowed upon us: evermore beseeching thy mercy, that like as thou dost grant

† Alleluia *is not added to these* ℣℣. *and* ℞℞. *in Eastertide.*

the prayers of them that call upon thee, so thou wouldest not forsake them, but rather dispose their way towards the attainment of thy heavenly reward. Through Christ, our Lord. ℞. Amen.

TO INVOKE THE HOLY SPIRIT.

Veni, Creator Spiritus.

(The first verse of this hymn is sung kneeling.)

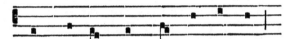

COME Hó - ly Ghost, Cre - á - tor blest.
Vouchsafe within our souls to rest;
Come with thy grace and heavenly aid,
And fill the hearts which thou hast made.

(All stand.)

To thee, the Comforter, we cry,
To thee, the gift of God most high,
The fount of life, the fire of love,
The soul's anointing from above.

O finger of the hand divine,
The sevenfold gifts of grace are thine ;
True promise of the Father thou,
Who dost the tongue with power endow.

Thy light to every sense impart,
And shed thy love in every heart ;
Thine own unfailing might supply
To strengthen our infirmity.

Drive far away our ghostly foe,
And thine abiding peace bestow ;
If thou be our preventing guide,
No evil can our steps betide.

Grant us through thee, O Holy One,
To know the Father and the Son ;
And this be our unchanging creed,
That thou dost from them both proceed.

All praise be thine, O risen Lord,
From death to endless life restored :
All praise to God the Father be
And Holy Ghost eternally.   Amen.

℣. Send forth thy Spirit and they shall be made.

(Alleluia *is not added in* E.T.)

℟. And thou shalt renew the face of the earth.

Let us pray.   *Collect.*

GOD, who didst teach the hearts of thy faithful people by the sending to them the light of thy Holy Spirit : grant us by the same Spirit to have a right judgment in all things, and evermore to rejoice in his holy comfort. Through Christ, our Lord. ℟. Amen.

PRAYER FOR ENGLAND.

The following prayer is to be recited at the principal Benediction on Sundays and Holy Days of Obligation, at latest before the **Tantum ergo;** *except on the second Sunday of every month, when the two Prayers given on page 236 should be recited in its place.* *

O BLESSED Virgin Mary, Mother of God, and our most gentle Queen and Mother, look down in mercy upon England, thy Dowry, and upon us all who greatly hope and trust in thee.

By thee it was that Jesus, our Saviour and our hope, was given unto the world ; and he has given thee to us that we may hope still more. Plead for us thy children, whom thou didst receive and accept at the foot of the Cross, O sorrowful Mother!

Intercede for our separated brethren, that with us in the one true fold they may be united to the chief Shepherd, the Vicar of thy Son. Pray for us all, dear Mother, that by faith fruitful in good works we may be counted worthy to see and praise God, together with thee, in our heavenly home. ℟. Amen.

· * *In the Counties of London (south of the Thames), of Kent, Sussex and Surrey, the Prayer O blessed Virgin is to be said at every Benediction on all Sundays and Holy Days of Obligation, and on the second Sunday in the month is to follow the two Prayers given below.*

On the second Sunday in the Month:

To Beg the Prayers of the Saints.

Hail Mary, etc.

O MERCIFUL God, let the glorious intercession of thy Saints assist us; above all, the most blessed Virgin Mary, Mother of thy only-begotten Son, and thy holy Apostles, Peter and Paul, to whose patronage we humbly recommend this our land. Be mindful of our fathers, Eleutherius, Celestine and Gregory, bishops of the holy City; of Augustine, Columba and Aidan, who delivered to us inviolate the faith of the holy Roman Church. Remember our holy martyrs, who shed their blood for Christ; especially our first martyr, Saint Alban, and thy most glorious bishop, Saint Thomas of Canterbury. Remember all those holy confessors, bishops and kings, all those holy monks and hermits, all those holy virgins and widows, who made this once an island of Saints, illustrious by their glorious merits and virtues. Let not their memory perish from before thee, O Lord, but let their supplication enter daily into thy sight; and do thou, who didst so often spare thy sinful people for the sake of Abraham, Isaac and Jacob, now, also, moved by the prayers of our fathers reigning with thee, have mercy upon us, save thy people, and bless thy inheritance; and suffer not those souls to perish, which thy Son hath redeemed with his own most precious blood. Who liveth and reigneth with thee, world without end. ℟. Amen.

Let us pray.

O MOST loving Lord Jesus, who, when thou wert hanging on the Cross, didst commend us all in the person of thy disciple John to thy most sweet Mother, that we might find in her our refuge, our solace and our hope; look graciously upon our beloved land, and on those who are bereaved of so powerful a patronage; that, acknowledging once more the dignity of this holy Virgin, they may honour and venerate her with all affection of devotion, and own her as Queen and Mother. May her sweet name be lisped by little ones, and linger on the lips of the aged and the dying; and may it be invoked by the afflicted, and hymned by the joyful; that this Star of the Sea being their protection and their guide, all may come to the harbour of eternal salvation. Who livest and reignest, world without end. ℞. Amen.

PRAYER FOR WALES.

The following prayer is to be said in the Principality of Wales at Benediction on Sundays and Holy Days of Obligation.

Let us pray.

O ALMIGHTY God, who in thine infinite goodness hast sent thine only-begotten Son into this world to open once more the gates of heaven, and to teach us how to know, love and serve thee, have mercy on thy people who dwell in Wales. Grant to them the precious gift of faith, and unite them in the one true Church founded by thy divine

Son ; that, acknowledging her authority and obeying her voice, they may serve thee, love thee, and worship thee as thou desirest in this world, and obtain for themselves everlasting happiness in the world to come. Through the same Jesus Christ, our Lord. ℟. Amen.

Our Lady, Help of Christians, pray for Wales.

St. David, pray for Wales.

St. Winefride, pray for Wales.

PRAYER FOR THE THREE DAYS FOLLOWING THE FEAST OF CORPUS CHRISTI.

MOST loving Jesus, who didst come into the world to enrich every soul with the life of thy grace, we thank thee that thou dost preserve and nourish that life in thy servants by giving thyself day by day, in the most holy Sacrament of the Eucharist, to be the remedy that shall heal their sickness, and the food that shall support their infirmity. And we humbly ask of thy goodness, that thou wouldst pour out upon them thy Holy Spirit, to fill them with the fullness of his power. May those who are defiled by mortal sin return to the same life of grace, now lost through their transgression ; may those who, of thy merciful bounty, are true even now to thy service, come daily to this thy feast with devout hearts, as thou shalt enable them. In the strength of that heavenly Food, may they be armed against the poison of their daily venial offences, and nourish evermore this life of grace within them, till at last, being cleansed more and more from their iniquities, they attain everlasting happiness in the world to come. ℟. Amen.

FORM OF CONSECRATION TO THE MOST SACRED HEART OF JESUS.

To be said on the Feast of Christ the King.

O JESUS, most gracious Redeemer of mankind, look upon us bowed in humble supplication at thy altar. Thine we are, and thine we would ever be ; to-day we desire to make that union still closer, dedicated, each of us, by a free choice to the service of thy most sacred Heart.

Many souls there are that never knew thee ; many have despised thy teaching and neglected thee ; have mercy, O Jesus, who art so rich in mercy, both on these and those, and let thy sacred Heart gather them all in. Be king, O Lord, not only over the faithful who have never wandered from home, but over the prodigal sons who have parted from thee ; make them return with all speed to their Father's house, lest they perish through want and bitterness of soul. Be king over those who have been led astray by false teaching, or are divided from us by schism, bringing them back within the sheltering walls of thy truth, and the unity of faith, that soon there may be one fold and one shepherd ; be king over those, also, who are sunk in the superstition of the Gentiles, or who follow the doctrine of the False Prophet, forbearing not to bring them too into the light and kingdom of God. Look down in mercy upon that race which once was called thy chosen people; and whereas of old they did accept the guilt of our Saviour's precious blood, may that blood now wash away their sins and bring them to eternal life.

Grant safety, Lord, and abiding liberty to thy Church; grant to all nations peace in the observing of due order. Praise to the divine Heart by which our salvation was achieved, glory and honour be given to it, now and world without end. ℞. Amen.

LITANY OF THE SACRED HEART.

KYRIE, eléison.   *or,* Lord, have mercy.
Christe, eléison.   *or,* Christ, have mercy.
Kyrie, eléison.   *or,* Lord, have mercy.
O Christ, hear us.
O Christ, graciously hear us.
O God the Father, of heaven, *Have mercy upon us.*
O God the Son, Redeemer of the world,
O God the Holy Ghost,
Holy Trinity, One God,
Heart of Jesus, Son of the eternal Father,
Heart of Jesus, formed by the Holy Ghost in the womb of the Virgin Mary,
Heart of Jesus, united in substance with the Word of God,
Heart of Jesus, of infinite majesty,
Heart of Jesus, holy temple of God,
Heart of Jesus, tabernacle of the most High,
Heart of Jesus, house of God and gate of heaven,
Heart of Jesus, burning furnace of charity,
Heart of Jesus, treasury of righteousness and love,

Heart of Jesus, full of goodness and love,
Heart of Jesus, abyss of all virtues,
Heart of Jesus, most worthy of all praise,
Heart of Jesus, King and centre of all hearts,
Heart of Jesus, in whom are all the treasures of wisdom and knowledge,
Heart of Jesus, in whom dwelleth all the fullness of the Godhead,
Heart of Jesus, in whom the Father was well pleased,
Heart of Jesus, of whose fullness we have all received,
Heart of Jesus, desire of the eternal hills,
Heart of Jesus, long-suffering and of great mercy,
Heart of Jesus, rich unto all that call upon thee,
Heart of Jesus, fount of life and holiness,
Heart of Jesus, propitiation for our sins,
Heart of Jesus, overwhelmed with reproaches,
Heart of Jesus, bruised for our transgressions,
Heart of Jesus, made obedient unto death,
Heart of Jesus, pierced by the spear,
Heart of Jesus, fount of all consolation,
Heart of Jesus, our life and resurrection,
Heart of Jesus, our peace and reconciliation,
Heart of Jesus, Victim for sinners,
Heart of Jesus, salvation of those who hope in thee.
Heart of Jesus, hope of those who die in thee,
Heart of Jesus, delight of all the Saints,
O Lamb of God that takest away the sins of the world,

Spare us, O Lord.

O Lamb of God, that takest away the sins of the
world,

Hear us, O Lord.

O Lamb of God, that takest away the sins of the
world,

Have mercy upon us.

℣. Jesu, meek and lowly of heart.

℞. Make our hearts like unto thy Heart.

Let us pray.

ALMIGHTY and everlasting God, look upon the
Heart of thy well-beloved Son, and upon the
praises and satisfactions which he rendered unto
thee in the name of sinners ; and to those who
seek thy pity do thou mercifully grant forgiveness,
in the name of the same thy Son Jesus Christ : Who
liveth and reigneth with thee, world without end.
℞. Amen.

ACT OF REPARATION
to be said
On the Feast of the Sacred Heart.

O SWEET Jesus, whose overflowing charity for
men is requited by so much forgetfulness,
negligence and contempt, behold us prostrate
before thy altar, eager to repair by a special act of
homage the cruel indifference and injuries, to
which thy loving Heart is everywhere subject.

Mindful alas ! that we ourselves have had a
share in such great indignities, which we now
deplore from the depths of our hearts, we humbly

ask thy pardon and declare our readiness to atone by voluntary expiation not only for our own personal offences, but also for the sins of those, who, straying far from the path of salvation, refuse in their obstinate infidelity to follow thee, their Shepherd and Leader, or, renouncing the vows of their baptism, have cast off the sweet yoke of thy law.

We are now resolved to expiate each and every deplorable outrage committed against thee; we are determined to make amends for the manifold offences against Christian modesty in unbecoming dress and behaviour, for all the foul seductions laid to ensnare the feet of the innocent, for the frequent violation of Sundays and holidays, and the shocking blasphemies uttered against thee and thy Saints.

We wish also to make amends for the insults to which thy Vicar on earth and thy Priests are subjected, for the profanation, by conscious neglect or terrible acts of sacrilege of the very Sacrament of thy divine love; and lastly for the public crimes of nations who resist the rights and the teaching authority of the Church which thou hast founded.

Would, O divine Jesus, we were able to wash away such abominations with our blood ! We now offer, in reparation for these violations of thy divine honour, the satisfaction thou didst once make to thy eternal Father on the Cross and which thou dost continue to renew daily on our altars; we offer it in union with the acts of atonement of

thy Virgin Mother and all the Saints and of the
pious faithful on earth ; and we sincerely promise
to make recompense, as far as we can with the help
of thy grace, for all neglect of thy great love and
for the sins we and others have committed in the
past.

Henceforth we will live a life of unwavering
faith, of purity of conduct, of perfect observance
of the precepts of the Gospel and especially that
of charity.

We promise to the best of our power to prevent others from offending thee and to bring as
many as possible to follow thee.

O loving Jesus, through the intercession of the
Blessed Virgin Mary, our model in reparation, deign
to receive the voluntary offering we make of this
act of expiation ; and by the crowning gift of per-
severance keep us faithful unto death in our duty
and the allegiance we owe to thee, so that we may
all one day come to that happy home, where thou
with the Father and the Holy Ghost livest and
reignest God, world without end. ℟. Amen.

THE HOLY ROSARY.

*From October 1st to November 2nd inclusive,
either during Mass or before the Blessed Sacrament exposed, five decades of the Rosary should be
recited, concluding with the prayers below, and
followed by the Litany of the B.V. Mary, page 226,
and the Prayer to St. Joseph, page 245.*

At other times, when the Rosary is publicly recited, it should conclude with the prayers below.

HAIL, holy Queen, Mother of mercy, hail, our life, our sweetness, and our hope! To thee do we cry, poor banished children of Eve ; to thee do, we send up our sighs, mourning and weeping in this vale of tears. Turn, then, most gracious advocate, thine eyes of mercy towards us ; and after this our exile show unto us the blessed fruit of thy womb, Jesus. O clement, O loving, O sweet Virgin Mary.

℣. Pray for us, O holy Mother of God.

℟. That we may be made worthy of the promises of Christ.

Let us pray.

O GOD, whose only-begotten Son, by his life, death and resurrection, hath purchased for us the rewards of eternal life : grant, we beseech thee, that, meditating upon these mysteries in the most holy Rosary of the Blessed Virgin Mary, we may both imitate what they contain, and obtain what they promise. Through the same Christ, our Lord. ℟. Amen.

PRAYER TO ST. JOSEPH.

To be said after the Rosary and Litany during the month of October.

O BLESSED Joseph, we come to thee for refuge in our tribulations. We have asked help of that most holy Virgin who was betrothed to thee, and now we appeal, with the same confidence, for thy advocacy. We entreat thee by that intimate affection, which united thee to the sinless Virgin Mother of God, by that fatherly love, with which thou didst take the Child Jesus in thy arms, to look down in mercy on the inheritance which the same Jesus Christ hath bought with his precious blood, and to lend us thy powerful aid in our necessities.

Ever-watchful guardian of the Holy Family, protect the chosen people of Jesus Christ. Most loving father, preserve us from all infection of false doctrine and corrupt manners. Most powerful champion, enthroned high in heaven, take part with us in this warfare against the powers of darkness ; and as thou didst rescue the Child Jesus, when his life was threatened of old, so now do thou defend God's holy Church from the malicious devices of the enemy, and from all adversity. Keep us, one and all, in thy abiding protection, going before us as our example and our patron ; that we may live a life of holiness, die a holy death, and attain everlasting happiness in the world to come. Ry. Amen.

PRAYERS

to be recited according to the direction of the Bishop.

FOR THE HARVEST.

Let us pray for the harvest and the industries of our country :

O ALMIGHTY God, we beseech thy mercy that thou wouldst ripen with thy blessing the fruits of the earth which thou hast created. Grant that thy people may be ever grateful for thy gifts, and fill with all good things the souls of them that hunger ; that rich and poor may praise thy glorious name. Through Christ, our Lord ℟. Amen.

℣. Vouchsafe, O Lord, to give and preserve the fruits of the earth.

℟. We beseech thee, hear us.

℣. Vouchsafe, O Lord, to bless the industries of the country.

℟. We beseech thee, hear us.

Our Father. Hail Mary.

IN THANKSGIVING FOR THE HARVEST.

Let us return thanks to God for all the mercies he has shown to us, especially for the harvest :

O GOD, whose mercies are without number, and the treasures of thy goodness inexhaustible, we render thanks to thy most gracious majesty for the gifts we have received, evermore entreating thy compassion : that as thou didst grant these favours we have asked of thee, so thou wouldst never forsake us, but prepare our hearts for a recompense in the world to come. Through Christ, our Lord. ℟. Amen.

Our Father. Hail Mary.

PRAYER FOR PEACE.

GIVE peace in our time, O Lord; because there is none other that fighteth for us, but only thou, O God.

℣. Peace be within thy walls.

℟. And plenteousness within thy palaces.

Let us pray.

O GOD, from whom all holy desires, all good counsels, and all just works do proceed : give unto thy servants that peace which the world cannot give ; that both, our hearts may be set to obey thy commandments, and also that by thee we, being defended from the fear of our enemies, may pass our time in rest and quietness. Through Christ, our Lord. ℞. Amen.

ASPERGES

On Sunday

before the principal Mass, the Priest who is to cele-brate, vested in a cope of the colour of the Office, goes to the Altar, and there, kneeling at the steps with the ministers, even in Eastertide, he receives from the Deacon the sprinkler and first sprinkles the Altar thrice, then himself, and rises and sprinkles the min-isters, beginning the Antiphon, **Thou shalt purge me,** *and the Choir continues :* **O Lord, with hyssop, etc.,** *as below. Meanwhile the Celebrant sprinkles the Clergy, then the people, saying in a low voice, with the ministers, the Psalm* **Miserere mei, Deus.**

ANTIPHON.

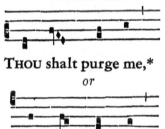

THOU shalt purge me,*

or

THOU shalt purge me,*

O Lord, with hyssop, and I shall be clean : thou shalt wash me, and I shall be whiter than snow. *Ps.* 51. Have mercy upon me, O God, after thy great goodness. ℣. Glory be to the Father.

And the Antiphon is repeated, **Thou shalt purge me.**

This Antiphon is said in the aforementioned manner at the sprinkling of holy Water on Sundays throughout the year, except on Passion Sunday and

Palm Sunday on which **Glory be** *is not said, but after
the Psalm* **Miserere mei** *the Antiphon* **Thou shalt
purge me** *is at once repeated. Excepting also in
Eastertide, that is from Easterday to Pentecost,
inclusive, at which season the following Antiphon is
chanted:*

ANTIPHON.

I   be- held   wá- ter, *
issuing out from the temple, on the right side,
alleluia : and all to whom that water came were
saved, and they shall say : alleluia, alleluia.

Ps. 118.   O give thanks unto the Lord, for he
is gracious: because his mercy endureth for ever.
℣.   Glory be.

The Antiphon is repeated, **I beheld water.**

On Trinity Sunday, the Antiphon **Thou shalt
purge me,** *is resumed as above.*

*On the holy days of Easter and Pentecost, where
there is a baptismal Font, the sprinkling is done with
water blessed the day before in the Font of Baptism,
and taken before the infusion of the Oil and Chrism.*

*The Antiphon being concluded in the afore-
mentioned manner, the Priest who has sprinkled the
water returns to the Altar, and, standing before the
steps of the Altar with joined hands, shall say:*

℣. O Lord, shew thy mercy upon us. (*E.T.*
Alleluia).

℟. And grant us thy salvation. (*E.T.*
Alleluia.)

℣. O Lord, hear my prayer.

℟. And let my cry come unto thee.

℣. The Lord be with you.

℟. And with thy spirit.

Let us pray.   *Collect.*

GRACIOUSLY hear us, O Lord holy Father
almighty, everlasting God : and vouchsafe to
send thy holy Angel from heaven; to guard and
cherish, protect, visit and defend all who dwell in
this dwelling-place.   Through Christ, our Lord.
℟. Amen.

PRAYER FOR THE QUEEN

after the chief Mass on all Sundays.

During or immediately after the last Gospel, according to custom, the following Antiphon shall be sung :

Domine, salvam fac reginam Elizabeth.

O LORD, save *Elizabeth* our queen, and mercifully hear us in the day when we call upon thee.

Then the Priest, standing at the foot of the Altar with the Ministers, their maniples being first removed, shall sing in the ferial tone the following :

Let us pray.   *Collect.*

WE beseech thee, almighty God, that thy servant *Elizabeth* our Queen, who by thy mercy hath received the government of this realm, may likewise receive an increase of every virtue: that being meetly adorned therewith she may flee from sin and iniquity, (*In time of war:* may overcome her enemies), and by thy grace may attain with Prince Philip and their royal offspring to thee, who art the way, the truth and the life. Through Christ, our Lord. ℟ Amen.

PRAYERS FOR THE CHURCH.

To be said kneeling after Low Mass for the Church in Russia.

The following is said thrice :

HAIL, MARY, full of grace; the Lord is with thee : blessed art thou among women, and blessed is the fruit of thy womb, Jesus. Holy

Mary, Mother of God, pray for us sinners, now and at the hour of our death. Amen.

Then the Priest begins, and all continue:

HAIL, Holy Queen, Mother of Mercy; hail, our life, our sweetness and our hope! To thee do we cry, poor banished children of Eve. To thee do we send up our sighs, mourning and weeping in this vale of tears. Turn then, most gracious Advocate, thine eyes of mercy towards us. And after this our exile shew unto us the blessed fruit of thy womb, Jesus. O clement, O loving, O sweet Virgin Mary.

℣. Pray for us, O holy Mother of God.

℟. That we may be made worthy of the promises of Christ.

Let us pray.

O GOD, our refuge and our strength, look down in mercy on thy people who cry to thee; and by the intercession of the glorious and Immaculate Virgin Mary, Mother of God, of Saint Joseph her Spouse, of thy blessed Apostles Peter and Paul, and of all the Saints, in mercy and goodness hear our prayers for the conversion of sinners, and for the liberty and exaltation of our holy Mother the Church. Through the same Christ, our Lord. ℟. Amen.

HOLY MICHAEL, Archangel, defend us in the day of battle; be our safeguard against the wickedness and snares of the devil: may God

rebuke him, we humbly pray; and do thou, Prince
of the heavenly host, by the power of God thrust
down to hell Satan and all wicked spirits who
wander through the world for the ruin of souls.
℞. Amen.

Then is said thrice:

Most Sacred Heart of Jesus.

℞. Have mercy on us.

PRAYERS FOR THE DEPARTED.

PSALM 130. *De profundis.*

OUT of the deep have I called unto thee,
O Lord : * Lord, hear my voice.

O let thine ears consider well : * the voice of
my complaint.

If thou, Lord, wilt be extreme to mark what
is done amiss : * O Lord, who may abide it?

For there is mercy with thee : * therefore shalt
thou be feared.

I look for the Lord, my soul doth wait for
him : * in his word is my trust.

My soul fleeth unto the Lord : * before the
morning watch, I say, before the morning watch.

O Israel, trust in the Lord, for with the Lord
there is mercy : * and with him is plenteous
redemption.

And he shall redeem Israel : * from all his
sins.

Rest eternal : * grant unto them, O Lord.

And let light perpetual : * shine upon them.

Our Father (*secretly*).

℣.   And lead us not into temptation.

℞.   But deliver us from evil.

℣.   From the gate of hell.

℞.   Deliver their souls, O Lord.

℣.   May they rest in peace.

℞.   Amen.

℣.   O Lord, hear my prayer.

℞.   And let my cry come unto thee.

℣.   The Lord be with you.

℞.   And with thy spirit.

Let us pray.   *Collect.*

O GOD, the Creator and Redeemer of all the faithful : grant unto the souls of thy servants and handmaids the remission of all their sins : that through devout supplications they may obtain the pardon which they have alway desired : Who livest and reignest, world without end.   ℞. Amen.

NOTE

CONCERNING THE CONCLUSION OF COLLECTS.

1. *In the Mass and Divine Office the longer ending is always used, viz.*, Through (the same) Jesus Christ thy Son our Lord : Who liveth and reigneth with thee in the unity of the (same) Holy Ghost, ever one God (*or* God, throughout all ages), world without end.

If the Collect be addressed to God the Son, it concludes: Who livest and reignest with God the Father in the unity . . . . ., etc., *as above.*

2. *Outside the Mass and Divine Office the shorter ending is used, viz.,* Through Christ, our Lord; *or (if the Collect be addressed to God the Son)*: Who livest and reignest, world without end (*or* for ever and ever).

LAUS DEO.

ALPHABETICAL INDEX

Lightning Source UK Ltd.
Milton Keynes UK
UKOW05n2021110517

300991UK00001B/1/P